# *The Elements* of **Java**™ *Style*

## SIGS Reference Library

Additional Volumes in Preparation

Rogue Wave
SOFTWARE

# *The Elements* of **Java**™ *Style*

Al Vermeulen
Scott W. Ambler
Greg Bumgardner
Eldon Metz
Trevor Misfeldt
Jim Shur
Patrick Thompson

**CAMBRIDGE**
UNIVERSITY PRESS

SIGS
BOOKS

PUBLISHED BY THE PRESS SYNDICATE OF THE
UNIVERSITY OF CAMBRIDGE
The Pitt Building, Trumpington Street, Cambridge, United Kingdom

CAMBRIDGE UNIVERSITY PRESS
The Edinburgh Building, Cambridge CB2 2RU, UK
40 West 20th Street, New York, NY 10011-4211, USA
10 Stamford Road, Oakleigh, VIC 3166, Australia
Ruiz de Alarcon 13, 28014 Madrid, Spain
Dock House, The Waterfront, Cape Town 8001, South Africa

http://www.cambridge.org

Published in association with SIGS Books

First published 2000
Reprinted in 2000, 2001

Design and composition by David Van Ness
Cover design by Andrea Cammarata

Printed in the United States of America

A catalog record for this book is available from the British Library.

Library of Congress Cataloging in Publication data is on record with the publisher.

ISBN 0 521 777682   paperback

The authors would like to thank
our loved ones for enduring us
while we toiled away on this book.

# Table of Contents

# Preface

A T ROGUE WAVE, we sell C++ and Java software compo-
nents. We have always included source code with our
products. Customers often browse through the code to get a
feeling, not just for how it works, but for how to write good
software. As a result, we have always felt pressure—maybe
more pressure than most companies—to have good, consistent style throughout our source code.

As the company grew, making sure programmers were all following the same rules became difficult. To address this, our
founder and first programmer, Tom Keffer, wrote 35 pages
that explained how we write C++ code at Rogue Wave. We
passed the document around and made sure new hires got a
copy. It worked. When customers asked how we maintained
consistency in our coding, we told them about Tom's "C++
Design, Implementation, and Style Guide," and sent them a
copy. Word spread and we turned Tom's document into a
technical report. We sent out thousands of copies and
received terrific positive feedback.

When Java came along, we decided we needed a document
like the "C++ Guide." A note went out to our internal
javadev@roguewave.com mailing list soliciting rules for Java
use that we should be using. The resulting list of rules became
the first draft of the "Rogue Wave Java Style Guide."

As the list of rules grew, the style guide began to look more
and more like a real book. This time, we decided to publish
our guide instead of simply issuing another Rogue Wave technical report. To our amazement, the folks at Cambridge University Press thought this was a great idea, and *The Elements
of Java Style* was born.

One of the first reviewers of that original draft was Scott Ambler, current president of Ronin International (www.ronin-intl.com). Scott liked the idea of the book and suggested we check out the coding standards for Java he'd been distributing on the Web. We liked his standards a lot and decided we should work as a team. The result of combining Scott's standards and the Rogue Wave style document is this book.

## Audience

We wrote this book for anyone writing Java code, but especially for programmers who are writing Java as part of a team. For a team to be effective, everyone must be able to read and understand everyone else's code. Having consistent style conventions is a good first step!

We assume you already know the basics of Java and object-oriented programming.

# Acknowledgments

THIS BOOK was a team effort. The team extends far beyond the seven named authors. We'd like to thank those who reviewed and contributed to the original "Rogue Wave Java Style Guide" and the "Ambysoft Inc. Coding Standards for Java." This includes Jeremy Smith, Tom Keffer, Wayne Gramlich, Pete Handsman, and Cris Perdue.

This book would certainly never have happened without the help and encouragement of the folks at Cambridge University Press. Our editor, Lothlórien Homet, hooked the Rogue Wave people up with Scott Ambler and made it all happen with her gentle, yet persistent, prodding. Thanks Lothlórien!

# Introduction

THE SYNTAX OF A PROGRAMMING LANGUAGE tells you what code it is possible to write—what the machine will understand. Style tells you what you ought to write—what the humans reading the code will understand. Code written with a consistent, simple style will be maintainable, robust, and contain fewer bugs. Code written with no regard to style will contain more bugs. It may simply be thrown away and rewritten rather than maintained.

Our two favorite style guides are classics: Strunk and White's *The Elements of Style* and Kernighan and Plauger's *The Elements of Programming Style*. These small books work because they are simple—a list of rules, each containing a brief explanation and examples of correct, and sometimes incorrect, use. We followed the same pattern in this book.

This simple treatment—a series of rules—enabled us to keep this book short and easy to understand. The idea is to provide a clear standard to follow, so programmers can spend their time on solving the problems of their customers, instead of worrying about naming conventions and formatting.

# 1.
# General Principles

While it is important to write software that performs well, many other issues should concern the professional Java developer. All *good* software performs well. But *great* software, written with style, is predictable, robust, maintainable, supportable, and extensible.

## 1. Adhere to the style of the original.

When modifying existing software, your changes should follow the style of the original code.[1] Do not introduce a new coding style in a modification, and do not attempt to rewrite the old software just to make it match the new style. The use of different styles within a single source file produces code that is more difficult to read and comprehend. Rewriting old code simply to change its style may result in the introduction of costly yet avoidable defects.

## 2. Adhere to the Principle of Least Astonishment.

The *Principle of Least Astonishment* suggests you should avoid doing things that will surprise a user of your software. This implies the means of interaction and the behavior exhibited by your software must be predictable and consistent,[2] and, if not, the documentation must clearly identify and justify any unusual patterns of use or behavior.

To minimize the chances that a user will encounter something surprising in your software, you should emphasize the following characteristics in the design, implementation, and documentation of your Java software:

| | |
|---|---|
| **Simplicity** | Build simple classes and simple methods. Determine how much you need to do to meet the expectations of your users. |
| **Clarity** | Ensure each class, interface, method, variable, and object has a clear purpose. Explain where, when, why, and how to use each. |
| **Completeness** | Provide the minimum functionality that any reasonable user would expect to find and use. Create complete documentation; document all features and functionality. |
| **Consistency** | Similar entities should look and behave the same; dissimilar entities should look and behave differently. Create and apply standards whenever possible. |
| **Robustness** | Provide predictable documented behavior in response to errors and exceptions. Do not hide errors and do not force clients to detect errors. |

## 3. *Do it right the first time.*

Apply these rules to any code you write, not just code destined for production. More often than not, some piece of prototype or experimental code will make its way into a finished product, so you should anticipate this eventuality. Even if your code never makes it into production, someone else may still have to read it. Anyone who must look at your code will appreciate your professionalism and foresight at having consistently applied these rules from the start.

## 4. *Document any deviations.*

No standard is perfect and no standard is universally applicable. Sometimes you will find yourself in a situation where you need to deviate from an established standard.

Before you decide to ignore a rule, you should first make sure you understand why the rule exists and what the consequences are if it is not applied. If you decide you must violate a rule, then document why you have done so.

This is the *prime directive*.

1    Jim Karabatsos. "When does this document apply?" In "Visual Basic
     Programming Standards." (GUI Computing Ltd., 22 March 1996).
     Accessed online at http://www.gui.com.au/jkcoding.htm, Aug 1999.

2    George Brackett. "Class 6: Designing for Communication: Layout,
     Structure, Navigation for Nets and Webs." In "Course T525: Designing
     Educational Experiences for Networks and Webs." (Harvard Graduate
     School of Education, 26 August 1999). Accessed online at
     http://hgseclass.harvard.edu/t52598/classes/class6/, Aug 1999.

# 2.
# Formatting
# Conventions

## 5. *Indent nested code.*

One way to improve code readability is to group individual statements into block statements and uniformly indent the content of each block to set off its contents from the surrounding code.

If you generate code using a Java development environment, use the indentation style produced by the environment. If you are generating the code by hand, use two spaces to ensure readability without taking up too much space:

```
class MyClass {
··void function(int arg) {
····if (arg < 0) {
······for (int index = 0; index <= arg; index++) {
········// ...
······}
····}
··}
}
```

In addition to indenting the contents of block statements, you should also indent the statements that follow a label to make the label easier to notice:

```
void function(int arg) {
··loop:
····for (int index = 0; index <= arg; index++) {
······switch (index) {
```

```
········case 0:
··········//...
··········break loop; // exit the for statement
········default:
··········//...
··········break; // exit the switch statement
······}
····}
}
```

Locate the opening brace '{' of each block statement in the last character position of the line that introduced the block. Place the closing brace '}' of a block on a line of its own, aligned with the first character of the line that introduced the block. The following examples illustrate how this rule applies to each of the various Java definition and control constructs.

**Class definitions:**

```
public class MyClass {
  ...
}
```

**Inner class definitions:**

```
public class OuterClass {
  ...
  class InnerClass {
    ...
  }
  ...
}
```

**Method definitions:**

```
void method(int j) {
  ...
}
```

**Static blocks:**

```
static {
  ...
}
```

**For-loop statements:**

```
for (int i = 0; i <= j; i++) {
   ...
}
```

**If and else statements:**

```
if (j < 0) {
   ...
}
else if (j > 0) {
   ...
}
else {
   ...
}
```

**Try, catch, and finally blocks:**

```
try {
   ...
}
catch (Exception e) {
   ...
}
finally {
   ...
}
```

**Switch statements:**

```
switch (value) {
   case 0:
      ...
      break;
   default:
      ...
      break;
}
```

**Anonymous inner classes:**

```
button.addActionListener(
   new ActionEventListener() {
```

```
    public void actionPerformed() {
      ...
    }
  }
)
```

**While statements:**

```
while (++k <= j) {
  ...
}
```

**Do-while statements:**

```
do {
  ...
} while (++k <= j);
```

💡 If you are managing a development team, do not leave it up
to individual developers to choose their own indentation
amount and style. Establish a standard indentation policy for
the organization and ensure that everyone complies with this
standard.

Our recommendation of two spaces appears to be the most
common standard, although your organization may prefer
three or even four spaces.

## 6.  *Break up long lines.*

While a modern window-based editor can easily handle long
source code lines by scrolling horizontally, a printer must trun-
cate, wrap, or print on separate sheets any lines that exceed its
maximum printable line width. To ensure your source code is
still readable when printed, you should limit your source code
line lengths to the maximum width your printing environment
supports, typically 80 or 132 characters.

First, do not place multiple statement expressions on a single
line if the result is a line that exceeds your maximum allowable
line length. If two statement expressions are placed on one line:

```
double x = Math.random(); double y = Math.ran
dom(); // Too Long!
```

Then introduce a new line to place them on separate lines:

```
double x = Math.random();
double y = Math.random();
```

Second, if a line is too long because it contains a complex expression:

```
double length = Math.sqrt(Math.pow(Math.random(),
2.0) + Math.pow(Math.random(), 2.0)); // Too Long!
```

Then subdivide that expression into several smaller sub-expressions. Use a separate line to store the result produced by an evaluation of each subexpression into a temporary variable:

```
double xSquared = Math.pow(Math.random(),2.0);
double ySquared = Math.pow(Math.random(),2.0);
double length = Math.sqrt(xSquared+ySquared);
```

Last, if a long line cannot be shortened under the previous two guidelines, then break, wrap, and indent that line using the following rules:

### Step one

If the top-level expression on the line contains one or more commas:

```
double length = Math.sqrt(Math.pow(x, 2.0),Math
.pow(y,2.0)); // Too Long!
```

Then introduce a line break after each comma. Align each expression following a comma with the first character of the expression proceeding the comma:

```
double length = Math.sqrt(Math.pow(x,2.0),
                          Math.pow(y,2.0));
```

### Step two

If the top-level expression on the line contains no commas:

```
class MyClass {
  private int field;
```

```
   ...
   boolean equals(Object obj) {
     return this == obj || (obj instanceof MyClass
&& this.field == obj.field); // Too Long!
   }
   ...
 }
```

Then introduce a line break just before the operator with the lowest precedence or, if more than one operator of equally low precedence exists between each such operator:

```
class MyClass {
  private int field;
  ...
  boolean equals(Object obj) {
    return this == obj
            || (this.obj instanceof MyClass
                && this.field == obj.field);
  }
  ...
}
```

**Step three**

Reapply steps one and two, as required, until each line created from the original statement expression is less than the maximum allowable length.

## 7.   *Include white space.*

*White space* is the area on a page devoid of visible characters. Code with too little white space is difficult to read and understand, so use plenty of white space to delineate methods, comments, code blocks, and expressions clearly.

Use a single space to separate:

■  A right parenthesis ')' or curly brace '}' and any keyword that immediately follows, a keyword and any left parenthesis '(' or curly brace '{' that immediately follows, or a right parenthesis ')' and any left curly brace '{' that immediately follows:

```
for·(...)·{
  ...
}

while·(...)·{
  ...
}

do·{
  ...
}·while·(...);

switch·(...)·{
  ...
}

if·(...)·{
  ...
}
else·if·(...)·{
  ...
}
else·{
  ...
}

try·{
  ...
}
catch·(...)·{
  ...
}
finally·{
  ...
}
```

- Any binary operator, except for the "." qualification operator and the expression that proceeds and the expression that follows the operator:

```java
double length = Math.sqrt(x * x + y * y);
double xNorm = length > 0.0 ? (x / length) : x;
```

Use blank lines to separate:

- Each logical section of a method implementation:

```java
void handleMessage(Message messsage) {

    DataInput content = message.getDataInput();
    int messageType = content.readInt();

    switch (messageType) {

      case WARNING:
        ... do some stuff here ...
        break;

      case ERROR:
        ... do some stuff here ...
        break;

      default:
        ... do some stuff here ...
        break;
    }
}
```

- Each member of a class and/or interface definition:

```java
public class Foo {

    /**
     * Defines an inner class.
     */
    class InnerFoo {
      ...
    }
```

```
/**
 * The Bar associated with this Foo.
 */
private Bar bar;

/**
 * Construct a Foo with the specified Bar.
 */
Foo(Bar bar) {
  this.bar = bar;
}
}
```

■ Each class and interface definition in a source file:

```
/*
 * ... file description ...
 */

package com.company.xyz;

/**
 * ... interface description ...
 */
interface FooInterface {
  ...
}

/**
 * ... class description ...
 */
public class Foo implements FooInterface {
  ...
}
```

## 8. *Do not use "hard" tabs.*

Many developers use tab characters to indent and align their source code, without realizing the interpretation of tab characters varies across environments. Code that appears to possess the correct formatting when viewed in the original editing environment can appear unformatted and virtually unreadable when transported to an environment that interprets tabs differently.

**TIP** To avoid this problem, always use spaces instead of tabs to indent and align source code. You may do this simply by using the space bar instead of the tab key or by configuring your editor to replace tabs with spaces. Some editors also provide a "smart" indentation capability. You will need to disable this feature if it uses tab characters.

Your organization should set a common indentation size and apply it consistently to all its Java code as outlined in Rule #5.

# 3.

# Naming Conventions

THE FOLLOWING naming conventions are identical to those used by SUN MICROSYSTEMS in naming the identifiers that appear in the *Java Software Development Kit.*[3,4]

### 9. *Use meaningful names.*

When you name a class, variable, method, or constant, use a name that is, and will remain, meaningful to those programmers who must eventually read your code. Use meaningful words to create names. Avoid using a single character or generic names that do little to define the purpose of the entities they name.

The purpose for the variable "a" and the constant "65" in the following code is unclear:

```
if (a < 65) { // What property does 'a' describe?
  y = 65 - a; // What is being calculated here?
}
else {
  y = 0;
}
```

The code is much easier to understand when meaningful names are used:

```
if (age < RETIREMENT_AGE) {
  yearsToRetirement = RETIREMENT_AGE - age;
}
else {
  yearsToRetirement = 0;
}
```

The only exception to this rule concerns temporary variables whose context provides sufficient information to determine their purpose, such as a variable used as a counter or index within a loop:

```java
for (int i = 0; i < numberOfStudents; ++i) {
  enrollStudent(i);
}
```

Some variable meanings and use scenarios occur frequently enough to be standardized.

(See Rule #28 for more information.)

## 10. Use familiar names.

Use words that exist in the terminology of the target domain. If your users refer to their clients as customers, then use the name Customer for the class, not Client. Many developers will make the mistake of creating new or generic terms for concepts when satisfactory terms already exist in the target industry or domain.

## 11. Question excessively long names.

The name given an object must adequately describe its purpose. If a class, interface, variable, or method has an overly long name, then that entity is probably trying to accomplish too much.

Instead of simply giving the entity a new name that conveys less meaning, first reconsider its design or purpose. A refactoring of the entity may produce new classes, interfaces, methods, or variables that are more focused and can be given more meaningful yet simpler names.

## 12. Join the vowel generation.

Abbreviations reduce the readability of your code and introduce ambiguity if more than one meaningful name reduces to the same abbreviation.

Do not attempt to shorten names by removing vowels. This  practice reduces the readability of your code and introduces ambiguity if more than one meaningful name reduces to the same consonants.

The casual reader can understand the names in this definition:

```
public Message appendSignature(Message message,
                               String signature) {
    ...
}
```

While the shortened forms are more difficult to read:

```
public Msg appndSgntr(Msg msg,
                      String sgntr) {
    ...
}
```

If you remove vowels simply to shorten a long name, then you need to question whether the original name is appropriate. See Rule #11.

## 13. Capitalize only the first letter in acronyms.

This style helps to eliminate confusion in names where uppercase letters act as word separators, and it is especially important if one acronym immediately follows another:

```
setDSTOffset()          setDstOffset()

loadXMLDocument()       loadXmlDocument()
```

This rule does not apply to:

- Acronyms that appear within the name of a constant as these names only contain capital letters (see Rule #31):

  ```
  static final String XML_DOCUMENT = "text/XML";
  ```

- Acronyms that appear at the beginning of a method, variable or parameter name, as these names should always start with a lowercase letter (see Rules #22 and #25):

  ```
  private Document xmlDocument;
  ```

### 14. Do not use names that differ only in case.

The Java compiler can distinguish between names that differ only in case, but a human reader may fail to notice the difference.

For example, a variable named **theSQLInputStream** should not appear in the same scope as a variable named **theSqlInputStream**. If both names appear in the same scope, each effectively hides the other when considered from the perspective of a person trying to read and understand the code.[5]

## Package Names

### 15. Use the reversed, lowercase form of your organization's Internet domain name as the root qualifier for your package names.

Any package distributed to other organizations should include the lowercase domain name of the originating organization, in reverse order.[6] For example, if a company named ROGUE WAVE SOFTWARE, whose Internet domain name is roguewave.com, decides to distribute an application server package called `server`, then Rogue Wave would name that package `com.roguewave.server`.

SUN MICROSYSTEMS has placed restrictions on the use of the
package qualifier names java and javax. The java package
qualifier may only be used by Java vendors to provide con-
forming implementations of the standard Java class libraries.
SUN MICROSYSTEMS reserves the name javax for use in quali-
fying its own Java extension packages.

### 16. Use a single, lowercase word as the root name of each package.

The qualified portion of a package name should consist of a
single, lowercase word that clearly captures the purpose and
utility of the package. A package name may consist of a meaningful abbreviation. Examples of acceptable abbreviations are
the standard Java packages of java.io and java.net.

### 17. Use the same name for a new version of a package, but only if that new version is still binary compatible with the previous version, otherwise, use a new name.

The intent of this rule is to ensure that two Java classes with
identical qualified names will be binary and behaviorally
compatible with each other.

The Java execution model binds the clients of a class to
implementation of that class at run time. This means unless
you adopt this convention, you have no way to ensure that
your application is using the same version of the software you
had used and tested with when you built the application.

If you produce a new version of a package that is not binary
or behaviorally compatible, you should change the name of
the package. This renaming may be accomplished in a vari-
ety of ways, but the safest and easiest technique is simply to

add a version number to the package name and then incre-
ment that version number each time an incompatible change
is made:

```
com.roguewave.server.v1
com.roguewave.server.v2
:
```

The one drawback to this approach is the dependency
between a client of a package and a specific implementation
of that package is hard-coded into the client code. A package
client can only be bound to a new version of that package by
modifying the client code.

## Type Names

**18.** *Capitalize the first letter of each word that appears
in a class or interface name.*

The capitalization provides a visual cue for separating the
individual words within each name. The leading capital letter
provides a mechanism for differentiating between class or
interface names and variable names (see Rule #25):

```
public class PrintStream
  extends FilterOutputStream {
  ...
}
public interface ActionListener
  extends EventListener {
  ...
}
```

### Class Names.

**19.** *Use nouns when naming classes.*

Classes define objects, or *things,* which are identified by
nouns:

```
class CustomerAccount {
  ...
}
public abstract class KeyAdapter
  implements KeyListener {
  ...
}
```

## 20. Pluralize the names of classes that group related attributes, static services, or constants.

Give classes that group related attributes, static services, or constants a name that corresponds to the plural form of the attribute, service, or constant type defined by the class.

The java.awt.font.LineMetrics class is an example of a class that defines an object that manages a group of related attributes:

```
/**
 * The <code>LineMetrics</code> class gives
 * access to the metrics needed to layout
 * characters along a line and to layout of
 * a set of lines.
 */
public class LineMetrics {
  public LineMetrics()
  public abstract int getNumChars();
  public abstract float getAscent();
  public abstract float getDescent();
  public abstract float getLeading();
  public abstract float getHeight();
  ...
}
```

The java.beans.Beans class is an example of a class that defines a group of related static services:

```
/**
 * The <code>Beans</code> class provides some
 * general purpose beans control methods.
 */
```

```java
public class Beans {
  public static Object instantiate(...) {...}
  public static Object getInstanceOf(...) {...}
  public static boolean isInstanceOf(...) {...}
  public static boolean isDesignTime() {...}
  public static boolean isGuiAvailable() {...}
  public static void setDesignTime(...) {...}
  public static void setGuiAvailable(...) {...}
  ...
}
```

The `java.sql.Types` class is an example of a class that defines a group of related static constants:

```java
/**
 * The <code>Types</code> class defines constants
 * that are used to identify SQL types.
 */
public class Types {
  public final static int BIT = -7;
  public final static int TINYINT = -6;
  public final static int SMALLINT = 5;
  public final static int INTEGER = 4;
  public final static int BIGINT = -5;
  public final static int FLOAT = 6;
  public final static int REAL = 7;
  public final static int DOUBLE = 8;
  public final static int NUMERIC = 2;
  public final static int DECIMAL = 3;
  public final static int CHAR = 1;
  ...
}
```

### Interface Names

### 21. *Use nouns or adjectives when naming interfaces.*

An *interface* provides a declaration of the services provided by an object, or it provides a description of the capabilities of an object.

Use nouns to name interfaces that act as service declarations:

```
public interface ActionListener {
  public void actionPerformed(ActionEvent e);
}
```

Use adjectives to name interfaces that act as descriptions of capabilities. Most interfaces that describe capabilities use an adjective created by tacking an "able" or "ible" suffix onto the end of a verb:

```
public interface Runnable {
  public void run();
}

public interface Accessible {
  public Context getContext();
}
```

## Method Names

### 22. Use lowercase for the first word and capitalize only the first letter of each subsequent word that appears in a method name.

The capitalization provides a visual cue for separating the individual words within each name. The leading lowercase letter provides a mechanism for differentiating between a method invocation and a constructor invocation:

```
class MyImage extends Image {
  public MyImage() {
    ...
  }

  public void flush() {
    ...
  }

  public Image getScaledInstance() {
    ...
  }
}
```

### 23. Use verbs when naming methods.

Methods and operations commonly define *actions*, which are verbs.

```
class Account {
  private int balance;
  ...
  public void withdraw(int amount) {
    deposit(-1 * amount);
  }

  public void deposit(int amount) {
    this.balance += amount;
  }
}
```

### 24. Follow the JavaBeans™ conventions for naming property accessor methods.

The JavaBeans™ specification[7] establishes standard naming conventions[8] for methods that give access to the properties of a JavaBean implementation. You should apply these conventions when naming methods in any class, regardless of whether it implements a Bean.

A JavaBean exposes boolean properties using methods that begin with "is":

```
boolean isValid() {
  return this.isValid;
}
```

A JavaBean gives read access to other property types using methods that begin with "get":

```
String getName() {
  return this.name;
}
```

The accessor method for reading an indexed property takes an int index argument:

```
String getAlias(int index) {
  return this.aliases[index];
}
```

A JavaBean gives write access to boolean and other types of properties using methods that begin with "set":

```
void setValid(boolean isValid) {
  this.isValid = isValid;
}

void setName(String name) {
  this.name = name;
}
```

The accessor method for setting an indexed property takes an int index argument:

```
void setAlias(int index, String alias) {
  this.aliases[index] = alias;
}
```

The *Java Development Kit* strongly adheres to these conventions. The is/get/set notation is required for exposing the component properties of a Bean unless you define a BeanInfo class.[9,10]

## Variable Names

*25. Use lowercase for the first word and capitalize only
    the first letter of each subsequent word that appears
    in a variable name.*

The capitalization provides a visual cue for separating the individual words within each name. The leading lowercase letter provides a mechanism for differentiating between variable names and class names (see Rule #18):

```
class Customer {
  ...
  private Address address;
```

```
  private Phone daytimePhone;
  ...
  public Address setAddress(Address address) {
    Address oldAddress = this.address;
    this.address = address;
    return oldAddress;
  }
  ...
  public void setDaytimePhone(Phone daytimePhone);
    ...
  }
  ...
}
```

### 26. *Use nouns to name variables.*

Variables refer to objects, or *things,* which are identified by nouns:

```
class Customer {
  ...
  private Address    billingAddress;
  private Address    shippingAddress;
  private Phone      daytimePhone;
  private Vector     openOrders;
  ...
}
```

### 27. *Pluralize the names of collection references.*

Give fields and variables that refer to collections of objects a name that corresponds to the plural form of the object type contained in the collection. This enables a reader of your code to distinguish between variables representing multiple values from those representing single values:

```
Customer[] customers =
  newCustomer[MAX_CUSTOMERS];

void addCustomer(int index, Customer customer) {
  this.customers[index] = customer;
}
```

```
Vector orderItems = new Vector();

void addOrderItem(OrderItem orderItem) {
  this.orderItems.addElement(orderItem);
}
```

## 28. *Establish and use a set of standard names for trivial "throwaway" variables.*

You should use full descriptive names for most variables, but many variable types that appear frequently within Java code have common "shorthand" names, which you may choose to use instead.[11,12] The following table lists a few examples:

| Character | c, d, e |
| Coordinate | x, y, z |
| Exception | e |
| Graphics | g |
| Object | o |
| Stream | in, out, inOut |
| String | s |

## Field Names

## 29. *Qualify field variables with "`this`" to distinguish them from local variables.*

To make distinguishing between local variables and field variables easier, always qualify field variables using "`this`":

```
public class AtomicAdder {

  private int count;

  public AtomicAdder(int count) {
    this.count = count;
  }
```

```java
  public synchronized int fetchAndAdd(int value) {
    int temp = this.count;
    this.count += value;
    return temp;
  }

  public synchronized int addAndFetch(int value) {
    return this.count += value;
  }
}
```

## Parameter Names

*30. When a constructor or "set" method assigns a parameter to a field, give that parameter the same name as the field.*

While hiding the names of instance variables with local variables is generally poor style, in this case some benefits exist. Using the same name relieves you of the responsibility for coming up with a name that *is* different. Using the same name also provides a subtle clue to the reader that the parameter value is destined for assignment to the field of the same name.

```java
  class Dude {

    private String name;

    public Dude(String name) {
      this.name = name;
    }

    public setName(String name) {
      this.name = name;
    }
  }
```

# Constant Names

**31. Use uppercase letters for each word and separate each pair of words with an underscore when naming constants.**

The capitalization of constant names distinguishes them from other nonfinal variables:

```
class Byte {
  public static final byte MAX_VALUE = 255;
  public static final byte MIN_VALUE = 0;
  public static final Class TYPE = Byte.class;
}
```

3 Sun Microsystems. *Java™ Code Conventions*. (Palo Alto, California: Sun Microsystems Inc., 20 April 1999). Accessed online at ftp://ftp.javasoft.com/docs/codeconv/CodeConventions.pdf, Aug 1999.

4 Sun Microsystems. *Java™ 2 Platform, Standard Edition, v1.2.2 API Specification*. (Sun Microsystems Inc., 1999). Accessed online at http://java.sun.com/products/jdk/1.2/docs/api/index.html, Aug 1999.

5 Jonathan Nagler. "Coding Style and Good Computing Practices." *The Political Methodologist*, Vol. 6, No. 2 (Spring 1995). Accessed online at http://wizard.ucr.edu/~nagler/coding_style.html, Aug 1999.

6 James Gosling et al. *The Java™ Language Specification*. (Reading, Massachusetts: Addison–Wesley, 1996), pp. 125–126.

7 To be called "Java Beans" or "Beans" for the remainder of this book.

8 Sun Microsystems. *JavaBeans™ API Specification*., ed. Graham Hamilton, (Mountain View, California: Sun Microsystems Inc., 1997), pp. 54–57. Accessed online at http://www.javasoft.com/beans/docs/beans.101.pdf, Aug 1999.

9 Ibid., pp. 56–57.

10 Patrick Chan, and Rosanna Lee. *The Java™ Class Libraries, Volume 2: java.applet, java.awt, java.beans., 2nd Edition*. (Reading, Massachusetts: Addison–Wesley, 1998), pg. 132.

11 James Gosling et al. *The Java™ Language Specification*.

12 Sun Microsystems. *Java™ Code Conventions*.

# 4.
# Documentation
# Conventions

### 32. Write documentation for those who must use your code and those who must maintain it.

Document the public programming interface of your code so others can use it correctly and effectively. Document the private interface and internal implementation details of your code so others can maintain and enhance it.

Always assume someone who is completely unfamiliar with your code will eventually have to read and understand it. In fact, if enough time passes, your own code may become unfamiliar, so this person may even be you!

### 33. Keep comments and code in sync.

> When the code and the comments disagree, both are probably wrong.—*Norm Schryer, Bell Labs*

When you modify code, make sure you also update any related comments.[13] The code and documentation together form a software product, so treat each with equal importance.

### 34. Use the active voice and omit needless words.

Comments are a form of prose. Forceful, clear, and concise language is especially beneficial for technical documentation. Use it.

## Comment Types

Java supports three comment types:

■ A *documentation comment* that starts with "/**"and ends
with "*/":

```
/**
 * A documentation comment.
 */
```

■ A *standard,* or *C-style, comment,* which starts with "/*"
and ends with "*/":

```
/*
 * A standard comment.
 */
```

■ A *one-line,* or *end-line, comment* that begins with "//" and
continues through the end of the line.

```
// A one-line comment.

class MyClass {
  int myField; // An end-line comment.
  ...
}
```

Each comment type serves a particular purpose and you should
use each type in a manner consistent with that purpose.

### 35. Use documentation comments to describe the
###     programming interface.

You may place documentation comments in front of any
class, interface, method, constructor, or field declaration that
appears in your code. These comments provide information
the Javadoc utility uses to generate HTML-formatted class
reference or Application Programming Interface (API) documentation. To create this documentation, the Javadoc utility
reads these comments as it parses all the declarations that

appear in a set of Java source code files. This information is used by Javadoc to produce a corresponding set of HTML pages that describe, by default, all the public and protected classes, inner classes, interfaces, constructors, methods, and fields found in those files.[14]

Javadoc only recognizes documentation comments when they appear immediately before a class, interface, constructor, method, or field declaration. Javadoc ignores any documentation comments that appear within the body of a method, so do not use them in this manner. Javadoc allows only one documentation comment per declaration statement, so do not attempt to use more than one comment block per declaration.

The primary purpose for documentation comments is to define a *programming contract*[15] between a *client* and a supplier of a *service*. The documentation associated with a method should describe all aspects of behavior on which a caller of that method can rely and should not attempt to describe implementation details.

The following code illustrates the use of documentation comments to document a class that declares an inner-class, a field, a method, and a constructor:

```
/**
 * The <code>Rectangle2D</code> class describes
 * a rectangle defined by location (x,y) and
 * dimensions (w,h).
 * ...
 */
public abstract class Rectangle2D
  extends RectangularShape {

  /**
   * The <code>Double</code> class defines a
   * rectangle specified in double coordinates...
   */
  static class Double extends Rectangle2D {...}
   ...
```

```
/**
 * The bitmask that indicates that a point lies
 * below this Rectangle2D...
 */
static int OUT_BOTTOM;
...
/**
 * Adds a Rectangle2D to this Rectangle2D...
 */
public void add(Rectangle2D r) {...}
  ...
/**
 * This is an abstract class that cannot be
 * instantiated directly...
 */
protected Rectangle2D() {...}
  ...
}
```

### 36. *Use standard comments to hide code without removing it.*

Use standard C-style comments when you wish to hide code temporarily from the compiler without actually removing it from the source file. You may only use this comment type to "comment-out" a section of code that does not have another comment block embedded within it.

 To avoid any problems with nested comment blocks, because they look very much like documentation comments, you should not use this type of comment for any purpose other than for temporarily hiding code.

The following code fragment demonstrates how to use this comment type to hide a member function definition:

```
/**
 * ...
 * @deprecated
 */
```

```
/*
   I have temporarily removed this method because
   it has been deprecated for some time, and I
   want to determine whether any other packages
   are still using it! - J. Kirk on 9 Dec 1997

public void thisOldFunction() {
   // There has got to be a better way!
   ...
}
*/
```

### 37. Use one-line comments to explain implementation details.

Use one or more one-line comments to document:

- The purpose of specific variables or expressions.
- Implementation-level design decisions.
- The source material for complex algorithms.
- Defect fixes or workarounds.
- Code that may benefit from further optimization or elaboration.
- Known problems, limitations, or deficiencies.

Strive to minimize the need for embedded comments by writing code that documents itself. Do not add comments that simply repeat what the code does.[16] Add comments only if they add useful information:

```
double totalCost; // Used to total invoice.
...

// Apply the discount to all invoices over $1000.
if (totalCost > 1000.0) { // :TODO: Use constant?

   // The discount is hard-coded because current
   // customers all use the same discount rate.
```

```
    // We will need to replace this constant with a
    // variable if we ever get a customer who needs
    // a different rate, or one that wants to apply
    // multiple discount rates!

    totalCost = totalCost * DISCOUNT;
}
```

# Documentation Comments

## 38. Describe the programming interface before you write the code.

The best time to create API reference documentation is early in the development process. Use documentation or "doc" comments to define the purpose, use, and behavior of each class or interface that forms part of a potential design solution. Write these comments while the purpose and rationale for introducing the new type is still fresh in your mind. Do not think you must wait to complete the implementation of every method before generating documentation—the Javadoc utility can run on Java source files containing classes whose methods are simple stubs with no method bodies. This means you can write documentation comments and run Javadoc in the earliest stages of implementation, before writing any method bodies.[17]

The initial description of a type and its methods and fields should not only provide guidance to the developers who must implement that type, but also form the basis for the final API reference documentation for that type. A developer tasked with implementing a class may choose to elaborate on the original documentation when the implementation details of the public interface become better defined and more apparent.

### 39. Document public, protected, package, and private members.

Supply documentation comments for all members, including those with package, protected, and private access. This allows for the generation of detailed, implementation-level documentation.[18] The developer who must learn and understand your code before implementing an enhancement or bug fix will appreciate your foresight in providing quality documentation for all class members, not just for the public ones.

### 40. Provide a summary description and overview for each package.

The Javadoc utility provides a mechanism for including package descriptions in the documentation it generates. Use this capability to provide a summary description and overview for each package you create.

To create a description for a package, you must create a *package comment file*, named package.html, and place that file in the package directory along with the other package source files. Javadoc will automatically look for a filename in this location.

The package comment file contains HTML, not Java source code. The package description must appear within an HTML <body> element. Javadoc treats the first sentence or phrase that appears within the <body>...</body> tags as the summary description for the package, just as it does when processing normal documentation comments.

You may use any Javadoc tag within the package description, except for the {@link} tag. Any @see tags that appear in a package description must use fully qualified names.

### 41. Provide a summary description and overview for each application or group of packages.

The Javadoc utility provides a mechanism for including a package-independent overview description in the documentation it generates. Use this capability to provide an overview description for each application or group of related packages you create.

To create an overview description, you must create an *overview comment file*, that may be given any name that ends in ".html", such as overview.html. To include this file in your documentation, you must tell Javadoc where to find the file by using the -overview option.

The overview comment file contains HTML, not Java source code. The overview must appear within an HTML <body> element. Javadoc treats the first sentence or phrase that appears between the <body>...</body> tags as the summary description for the application or package group, just as it does when processing normal documentation comments.

You may use any Javadoc tag within the description, except for the {@link} tag. Any @see tags that appear in an overview description must use fully qualified names.

## Comment Style

The "doc" comment formatting conventions listed in this section closely follow the conventions adopted and published by SUN MICROSYSTEMS.[19]

### 42. Use a single consistent format and organization for all documentation comments.

A properly formatted documentation comment contains a description followed by one or more Javadoc tags.

Format each documentation comment as follows:

- Indent the first line of the comment to align the slash character of the start-comment symbol "/**" with the first character in the line containing the associated definition.

- Begin each subsequent line within an asterisk '*'. Align this asterisk with the first asterisk in the start-comment symbol.

- Use a single space to separate each asterisk from any descriptive text or tags that appear on the same line.

- Insert a blank comment line between the descriptive text and any Javadoc tags that appear in the comment block.

- End each documentation comment block with the asterisk in the end-comment symbol "*/" aligned with the other asterisks in the comment block:

```
/**
 * Descriptive text for this entity.
 *
 * @tag Descriptive text for this tag.
 */
```

The following rules specify additional guidelines for creating high-quality, maintainable documentation comments.

## 43. Wrap keywords, identifiers, and constants with <code>...</code> tags.

Nest keywords, package names, class names, interface names, method names, field names, parameter names, constant names, and constant values that appear in a documentation comment within HTML <code>...</code> mark-up tags:

```
/**
 * Allocates a <code>Flag</code> object
 * representing the <code>value</code> argument.
 * ...
 */
public Flag(boolean value) {...}
```

The <code>...</code> tags tell HTML browsers to render the content in a different style[20] than that of normal text, so these elements will stand out.

### 44. *Wrap code with* <pre>...</pre> *tags.*

Nest code that appears in a documentation comment within HTML <pre>...</pre> mark-up tags:

```
/**
 * ...
 * The following example uses a
 * <code>Class</code> object to print the class
 * name of an object:
 *
 * <pre>
 * void printClassName(Object o) {
 *    System.out.println("The class of "
 *                        + o
 *                        + " is "
 *                        + o.getClass().getName());
 * }
 * </pre>
 * ...
 */
public final class Class {...}
```

The <pre>...</pre> tags are used to tell HTML browsers to retain the original formatting, including indentation and line-ends, of the "preformatted" element.

### 45. *Consider marking the first occurrence of an identifier with a* {@link} *tag.*

Each package, class, interface, method, and field name that appears within a documentation comment may be converted into a hypertext link by replacing that name with an appropriately coded[21] {@link} tag:

```
/**
 * Allocates a <code>Flag</code> object
 * representing the <code>value</code> argument.
 * Use this form of constructor as an alternative
 * to the {@link #Flag(String)} form.
 * ...
 */
public Flag(boolean value) {...}

/**
 * Allocates a <code>Flag</code> object
 * representing the value <code>true</code> if
 * the string argument is not <code>null</code>
 * and is equal to the string "true".
 * Use this form of constructor as an alternative
 * to the {@link #Flag(boolean)} form.
 * ...
 */
public Flag(String s) {...}
```

Do not feel you must create links to every identifier that appears within a comment block. Creating a significant number of these links can quickly clutter a comment block with {@link} tags, making it hard to read and maintain the original source.

Create links only when the documentation associated with  the referenced element would truly be of interest or value to the reader. Do not create links for every occurrence of an identifier. If an identifier appears more than once, simply create a link for the first occurrence and mark any subsequent instances using the mark-up discussed in Rule #43. Also, some classes and methods are so commonly used by a proficient Java programmer, they do not warrant their own links—again, these identifiers should still be marked as indicated in Rule #43.

### 46. *Establish and use a fixed ordering for Javadoc tags.*

SUN MICROSYSTEMS recommends the following Javadoc tag ordering[22]:

- In classes and interface descriptions:

```
/**
 * Description.
 *
 * @author
 * @version
 *
 * @see
 * @since
 * @deprecated
 */
```

Consider including an @author and @version tag in every class or interface description.

List multiple @author tags in chronological order, with the class or interface creator listed first.

- In method descriptions:

```
/**
 * Description.
 *
 * @param
 * @return
 * @exception
 *
 * @see
 * @since
 * @deprecated
 */
```

Include a @param tag for every parameter. List multiple @param tags in parameter declaration order.

Include a @return tag if the method returns any type other than void.

Include an @exception tag for every *checked exception* listed in a throws clause. Include an @exception tag for every *unchecked exception* that a user may reasonably expect to catch. List multiple @exception tags in alphabetical order of the exception class names.

- In field descriptions:

```
/**
 * Description.
 *
 * @see
 * @since
 * @deprecated
 */
```

Sort multiple @see tags according to their "distance" from the current location, in terms of document navigation and name qualification. Order each group of overloaded methods according to the number of parameters each accepts, starting with the method that has the least number of parameters:

```
/**
 * ...
 * @see #field
 * @see #Constructor()
 * @see #Constructor(Type...)
 * @see #method()
 * @see #method(Type...)
 * @see Class
 * @see Class#field
 * @see Class#Constructor()
 * @see Class#Constructor(Type...)
 * @see Class#method()
 * @see Class#method(Type...)
 * @see package.Class
 * @see package.Class#field
 * @see package.Class#Constructor()
 * @see package.Class#Constructor(Type...)
 * @see package.Class#method()
 * @see package.Class#method(Type...)
```

```
 * @see package
 * @see <a href="URL#label">label</a>
 * @see "String"
 * ...
 */
```

## 47. Write in the third-person narrative form.

When describing the purpose and behavior of classes, interfaces, and methods, use third-person *pronouns*—such as "**they**" and "**it**"—and third-person *verb* forms—such as "**sets**" and "**gets**"—instead of second-person forms—such as "set" and "get."

Some of the third-person verb forms that commonly appear in API documentation include

| | | |
|---|---|---|
| adds | deallocates | removes |
| allocates | destroys | returns |
| computes | gets | sets |
| constructs | provides | tests |
| converts | reads | writes |

## 48. Write summary descriptions that stand alone.

The Javadoc utility uses the first sentence or phrase in a documentation comment as a summary description of the class, interface, method, or field that immediately follows the comment block. To locate the end of the summary description, Javadoc starts at the beginning of the comment block and searches for a period that is followed by a space, tab, or end-of-line, or a Javadoc tag, whichever comes first.

Because this text provides a summary description for some entity, it must present a clear, simple, and concise description of that entity. Do not rely on other sentences in the comment block to provide additional context or elaboration.

Consider the following example:

```
/**
 * Use this function sparingly!
 * Applies the Foo-Bar algorithm to this node.
 */
public void doFooBar() {...}
```

Processing this code with Javadoc produces the following summary description for the doFooBar method:

Use this function sparingly!

Reordering the comment block produces a superior summary sentence:

```
/**
 * Applies the Foo-Bar algorithm to this node.
 * Use this function sparingly!
 */
public void doFooBar() {...}
```

If the entity is an overloaded method, the summary description must differentiate that method from the other forms of the same method:

```
/**
 * Allocates a <code>Flag</code> object
 * representing the <code>value</code> argument.
 * ...
 */
public Flag(boolean value) {...}

/**
 * Allocates a <code>Flag</code> object
 * representing the value true if the
 * string argument is not null and is equal
 * to the string "true".
 * ...
 */
public Flag(String s) {...}
```

### 49. *Omit the subject in summary descriptions of actions or services.*

A summary description does not require a subject because the subject can be determined from the context in which the description appears.

The following descriptions incorrectly provide a redundant identification of the subject:

```
/**
 * This method applies the Foo-Bar
 * algorithm to this node.
 * ...
 */
public void doFooBar() {...}

/**
 * The <code>doFooBar</code> method applies the
 * Foo-Bar algorithm to this node.
 * ...
 */
public void doFooBar() {...}
```

The following description correctly omits the subject:

```
/**
 * Applies the Foo-Bar algorithm to this node.
 * ...
 */
public void doFooBar() {...}
```

### 50. *Omit the subject and the verb in summary descriptions of things.*

A summary description for a class, interface, or field that represents a "thing" does not require an explicit subject or verb, as the description needs only to identify an object. A subject is unnecessary because it can be determined from the context. A verb is unnecessary because it simply states the subject "is," "exists as," or "represents" some object.

The following example illustrates a description that contains
an unnecessary subject and verb[23]:

```
/**
 * A thread group represents a set of threads.
 * ...
 */
public class ThreadGroup {...}
```

Drop the subject and verb to obtain the correct form of summary description:

```
/**
 * A set of threads.
 * ...
 */
public class ThreadGroup {...}
```

### 51. Use "this" rather than "the" when referring to instances of the current class.

When describing the purpose or behavior of a method, use
"this" instead of "the" to refer to an object that is an instance
of the class defining the method:

```
/**
 * Returns a <code>String</code> representing the
 * value of the <code>Flag</code> object.
 * ...
 */
public String toString() {...}
```

```
/**
 * Returns a <code>String</code> representing the
 * value of this <code>Flag</code> object.
 * ...
 */
public String toString() {...}
```

## 52. *Do not add parentheses to a method or constructor name unless you want to specify a particular signature.*

A method or constructor reference should not include any parentheses unless the reference identifies an overloaded method or constructor and you wish to refer to a single form of the overloaded operation.

 Do not add an empty pair of parenthesis "()" to indicate a name refers to a method. This practice causes confusion if the name is associated with an overloaded method and one of the overloaded forms of that method takes no arguments.

Consider the following pair of overloaded methods, as defined by the java.lang.String class:

```
public class String {
  ...
  public String toLowerCase() {...}
  public String toLowerCase(Locale locale) {...}
  ...
}
```

If you use the identifier "toLowerCase()" to refer to any or all of the toLowerCase methods, then you will likely confuse those who read your documentation. Most likely, your users will think you meant the first form of the method, not either or all forms of it. Use parentheses only when you want to specify the exact signature of a method or constructor:

| | |
|---|---|
| toLowerCase | Refers to either or both forms of the method. |
| toLowerCase() | Refers only to the first form of the method. |
| toLowerCase(Locale) | Refers only to the second form of the method. |

## Comment Content

### 53. *Provide a summary description for each class, interface, field, and method.*

Every class, interface, field, and method should be proceeded by a documentation comment that contains at least one sentence that acts as a summary description of that entity.

### 54. *Fully describe the signature of each method.*

The documentation for each method should always include a description for each parameter, each checked exception, any relevant unchecked exceptions, and any return value. See Rule #46 for information about Javadoc tag ordering and use.

### 55. *Include examples.*

One of the easiest ways to explain and understand how to use software is by giving specific examples.

Try to include a simple example in each nontrivial class and method description. Use the HTML <pre>...</pre> tags to maintain the formatting of each example:

```
/**
 *  ...
 * If you are formatting multiple numbers, it is
 * more efficient to get the format just once so
 * the system does not have to fetch the
 * information about the local language and
 * country conventions multiple times:
 * <pre>
 *  DateFormat df = DateFormat.getDateInstance();
 *  for (int i = 0; i < a.length; ++i) {
 *     output.println(df.format(myDate[i]) + "; ");
 *  }
 * </pre>
```

```
 * To format a number for a different Locale,
 * specify the locale in the call to
 * <code>getDateInstance</code>:
 * <pre>
 *   DateFormat df;
 *   df = DateFormat.getDateInstance(Locale.US);
 * </pre>
 * ...
 */
public abstract class DateFormat extends Format {
   ...
}
```

## 56. Document preconditions, postconditions, and invariant conditions.

A *precondition* is a condition that must hold true before a method starts if this method is to behave properly. A typical precondition may limit the range of acceptable values for a method argument.

A *postcondition* is a condition that must hold true following the completion of a method if this method has behaved properly. A typical postcondition describes the state of an object that should result from an invocation of the method given an initial state and the invocation parameters.

An *invariant* is a condition that must always hold true for an object. A typical invariant might restrict the integer field vacationDays to a value between 0 and 25.

As preconditions, postconditions, and invariants are the assumptions under which you use and interact with a class, documenting them is important, especially if these conditions are too costly to verify using run-time assertions.

## 57. Document known defects and deficiencies.

Identify and describe any outstanding problems associated with a class or method. Indicate any replacements or workarounds that exist. If possible, indicate when the problem might be resolved.

While no one likes to publicize problems in his or her code, your colleagues and customers will appreciate the information. This information will give them the chance to implement a workaround or to isolate the problem to minimize the impact of future changes.

## 58. Document synchronization semantics.

The presence of the `synchronized` modifier in the signature of a method normally reveals whether that method serializes calling threads to protect the state of an object. A user can determine whether a method is synchronized by looking at the documentation generated by Javadoc because Javadoc will include the modifier as part of the signature of each method that is declared as synchronized.

Java also provides a second synchronization mechanism that applies to a block of code instead of an entire method. Methods that use this second mechanism may, in fact, be thread-safe, but the signature of these methods will not indicate this. In this situation, you must indicate these are internally synchronized methods within the documentation for each such method.

## Internal Comments

**59. *Add internal comments only if they will aid others in understanding your code.***

Avoid the temptation to insert comments that provide useless or irrelevant information:

```java
public int occurrencesOf(Object item) {
  // This turned out to be much simpler
  // than I expected. Let's Go Mets!!
  return (find(item) != null) ? 1 : 0;
}
```

Add comments only when they provide information that will help others understand how the code works:

```java
public int occurrencesOf(Object item) {
  // This works because no duplicates are allowed:
  return (find(item) != null) ? 1 : 0;
}
```

If an internal comment does not add any value, it is best to let the code speak for itself.

**60. *Describe* why *the code is doing what it does, not* what *the code is doing.***

Good code is self-documenting. Another developer should be able to look at well-written code and determine what it does.

For example, a quick examination of the following code reveals that the program appears to give a 5 percent discount when an invoice totals over a thousand dollars:

```java
if (this.invoiceTotal > 1000.0) {
  this.invoiceTotal = this.invoiceTotal * 0.95;
}
```

The following comment provides little additional information:

```java
// Apply a 5% discount to all invoices
// over a thousand dollars:
```

```
if (this.invoiceTotal > 1000.0) {
  this.invoiceTotal = this.invoiceTotal * 0.95;
}
```

After reading this code, a reasonable developer may still want to know:

> Why is the discount 5 percent?
> Who determined the discount and dollar amount?
> When or why would these amounts change?

Identify and explain any domain-specific knowledge that is required to understand code:

```
// This term corrects for the effects of Jupiter,
// Venus, and the flattening of the earth:
sigma += (c1 * Angle.sin(a1)
        + c2 * Angle.sin(Angle.minus(L1,F))
        + c3 * Angle.sin(a2) );
```

## 61. Avoid the use of end-line comments.

End-line comments, one-line comments appended to a line of working code, should be used with care. They can easily interfere with the visual structure of code. Modifications to a commented line of code may push the comment far enough to the right that line wrapping or horizontal scrolling must be employed before the comment can be seen within an editor. Some programmers try to improve the appearance of end-line comments by aligning them so they are left justified, only to find themselves constantly realigning the comments each time the code is modified. This is a waste of time.

Place one-line comments on a separate line immediately preceding the code to which they refer. The only exception to this rule involves local variable declarations whose descriptions are short enough that an end-line comment can describe them without producing an unacceptably long line of code.

## 62. *Explain local variable declarations with an end-line comment.*

If the description of a local variable is quite short, consider placing the description in a comment on the same line as the declaration:

```
int cur = 0; // Index of current pattern element
int prev = 0; // Index of previous pattern element
```

Do not worry about positioning the comment so it appears aligned with other end-line comments.

## 63. *Establish and use a set of keywords to flag unresolved issues.*

Establish a set of keywords for use in creating special comments that you and other developers can use to signal unresolved issues, which must eventually be dealt with before the code is considered complete. These comments should include a date and the initials of the person who raised the issue. The keywords should be chosen to minimize the chances that the same text may appear elsewhere within the code. In the following example, a pair of colons decorates the word "UNRESOLVED" to increase the likelihood that it is unique:

```
// :UNRESOLVED: EBW, 11 July 1999
// This still does not handle the case where
// the input overflows the internal buffer!!
while (everMoreInput) {
   ...
}
```

## 64. *Label closing braces in highly nested control structures.*

While you should generally avoid creating deeply nested control structures, you can improve the readability of such code by adding end-line comments to the closing braces of each structure:

```
for (i...) {
  for (j...) {
    while (...) {
      if (...) {
        switch (...) {
          ...
        } // end switch
      } // end if
    } // end while
  } // end for j
} // end for i
```

### 65. Add a "fall-through" comment between two **case** labels, if no **break** statement separates those labels.

When the code following a switch statement's case label does not include a break but, instead, "falls through" into the code associated with the next label, add a comment to indicate this was your intent. Other developers will either incorrectly assume a break occurs, or wonder whether you simply forgot to code one:

```
switch (command) {
  case FAST_FORWARD:
    isFastForward = true;
    // Fall through!
  case PLAY:
  case FORWARD:
    isForward = true;
    break;
  case FAST_REWIND:
    isFastRewind = true;
    // Fall through!
  case REWIND:
    isRewind = true;
    break;
  ...
}
```

Note that two adjacent labels do not require an intervening comment.

## 66. *Label empty statements.*

When a control structure, such as while or for loop, has an empty statement by design, add a comment to indicate this was your intent.

```java
// Strip leading spaces
while ((c = reader.read()) == SPACE);
    // Empty!
```

13  Brian Kernighan, and P. J. Plauger. *The Elements of Programming Style.* (New York: McGraw–Hill, 1988), pg. 118.

14  Sun Microsystems' Javadoc home page
    http://java.sun.com/products/jdk/javadoc/index.html.

15  Bertrand Meyer, *Object-Oriented Software Construction, 2nd Edition.* (Englewood Cliffs, New Jersey: Prentice Hall, Inc, 1997).

16  Brian Kernighan and P. J. Plauger. *The Elements of Programming Style.* (New York: McGraw–Hill, 1988), pg. 119.

17  Sun Microsystems' Javadoc home page:
    http://java.sun.com/products/jdk/javadoc/index.html.

18  The javadoc utility acquired the capability to generate documentation for protected and private members in version 1.1.2.

19  Sun Microsystems. *How to Write Doc Comments for Javadoc,* ed. Doug Kramer, (Sun Microsystems Inc., 1999). Accessed online at http://java.sun.com/products/jdk/javadoc/writingdoccomments.html, Aug 1999.

20  Using a fixed, instead of a proportional-width typeface and using a different color.

21  Sun's Javadoc documentation describing @link tag. Accessed online at http://java.sun.com/products/jdk/1.3/docs/tooldocs/solaris/javadoc.html, Aug 1999.

22  Sun Microsystems. *How to Write Doc Comments for Javadoc.*

23  Note: Sun Microsystems does not currently appear to follow this convention. The summary descriptions for most classes and interfaces in the Java API still include both a subject and a verb as of version 1.2.2.

# 5.
# Programming
# Conventions

### 67. *Consider declaring classes representing fundamental data types as* `final`.

Simple classes representing fundamental data types, such as a `ComplexNumber` class in an engineering package, find widespread use within their target domain. As such, efficiency can become an issue of some importance. Declaring a class as `final` allows its methods to be invoked more efficiently.

Of course, declaring your class as `final` will prohibit its use as a superclass. Nevertheless, there is seldom any reason to extend a class that implements a fundamental data type. In most such cases, object composition is a more appropriate mechanism for reuse.

### 68. *Build concrete types from native types and other concrete types.*

Each nonnative, nonconcrete type that appears in the interface of a concrete type introduces a new, potentially volatile dependency, effectively exposing every client of that concrete type to volatility in these other types.

Minimize the number of dependencies that a concrete class has on nonnative, nonconcrete types. A concrete type that is defined purely in terms of native types provides better isolation and stability than a concrete type built from other concrete types. This is especially important for classes that implement fundamental data types, as dependencies on these low-level classes tend to proliferate throughout an application.

Consider the public interface of the java.util.BitSet class:

```java
public final class BitSet ... {
    public BitSet() {...}
    public BitSet(int) {...}
    public void set(int) {...}
    public void clear(int) {...}
    public boolean get(int) {...}
    public void and(BitSet) {...}
    public void or(BitSet) {...}
    public void xor(BitSet) {...}
    public int hashCode() {...}
    public int size() {...}
    public boolean equals(Object) {...}
    public Object clone() {...}
    public String toString() {...}
}
```

This class uses five data types in its interface: BitSet, which is a self-reference, the primitive types int and boolean, and the Java native types Object and String. Because the BitSet interface uses stable, native Java types, little possibility exists that changes outside this class will affect this class or its clients.

## 69. Define small classes and small methods.

Smaller classes and methods are easier to design, code, test, document, read, understand, and use. Because smaller classes generally have fewer methods and represent simpler concepts, their interfaces tend to exhibit better cohesion.

💡
TIP
Try to limit the interface of each class to the bare minimum number of methods required to provide the necessary functionality. Avoid the temptation to add "convenience" forms of a method when only one general-purpose form will suffice.

All sorts of informal guidelines exist for establishing the maximum size of a class or method—use your best judgment. If a class or method seems too big, then consider refactoring that class or method into additional classes or methods.

## 70. Define subclasses so they may be used anywhere their superclasses may be used.

A subclass that changes or restricts the behavior of its ancestor class by overriding something is a specialization of that class, and its instances may have limited substitutability for the instances of its ancestor class. A specialization may not always be used anywhere the parent class could be used.

A subclass that is behaviorally compatible with its ancestor class is a subtype and its instances are fully substitutable for instances of its ancestor class. A subclass that implements a subtype does not override anything in its ancestor class; it only extends the services provided by that class. A subtype has the same attributes and associations as its supertype.

The following design principle addresses the question of substitutability[24,25]:

> **The Liskov Substitution Principle**
> Methods that use references to base classes must be able to use objects of derived classes without knowing it.[26]

According to this principle, the ability to substitute a derived class object for a superclass object is characteristic of good design. Such designs offer more stability and reliability when compared with designs that fail to uphold this principle. When a design adheres to this principle, it generally indicates the designer did a good job identifying the base abstractions and generalizing their interfaces.

Any design that requires code changes to handle the introduction of a newly derived class is a bad design. Whenever a  derived class violates the existing contract between its superclasses and their clients, it forces changes in the existing code. When a method accepts a superclass instance, yet uses the derived type of this instance to control its behavior, changes will be required for the introduction of each new derived class. Changes of this kind violate the Open–Closed Principle and are something to avoid.

> **The Open–Closed Principle**
> Software entities (Classes, Modules, Functions, and so forth) should be open for extension, but closed for modification.[27]

Consider the following example:

```
class Shape {
  ...
  public Shape getNext() { return this.next; }
  public int getDepth() { return this.depth; }
  ...
}

class Circle extends Shape {...}

class Rectangle extends Shape {...}

class Canvas {

  public void drawShapes(ShapeList list) {
    Shape shape = list.getNextShape();
    // Use null to detect end of list
    while (shape != null) {
      drawShape(shape);
      shape = list.getNextShape();
    }
  }

  public void drawShape(Shape shape) {
    // Use derived type to call relevant method
    if (shape instanceof Circle)
      drawCircle((Circle) shape);
    else if (shape instanceof Rectangle)
```

```
      drawRectangle((Rectangle) shape);
  }

  public void drawCircle(Circle circle) {...}

  public void drawRectangle(Rectangle circle) {
    ...
  }


class ShapeList {
  ...
  protected Shape first;
  protected int entries;

  public int getEntries() { this.entries; }

  public Shape getNextShape() {
    Shape temp = this.first;
    if (null != this.first) {
      this.first = temp.getNext();
      this.entries--;
    }
    // Returns null when empty
    return temp;
  }
  ...
}
```

These classes make up a simple drawing package where Shapes are stored in ShapeLists and passed to a Canvas for rendering. The drawShapes method of a Canvas object reads one Shape object at a time from a list and dispatches each to the appropriate draw method. The process continues until the getNextShape method returns a null value, indicating the list has been fully traversed.

Now, suppose our design calls for a DepthFilteredShapeList class that can filter out any Shapes whose depth value falls outside a specified target range:

```
class DepthFilteredShapeList
  extends ShapeList {

  protected int min;
  protected int max;

  public Shape getNextShape() {
    Shape temp = this.first;

    if (null != this.first) {
      this.first = temp.next;
      this.entries--;
      int depth = temp.getDepth();

      // Is the shape in range?
      if (this.min > depth || depth > this.max) {
        // No - return null instead
        temp = null;
      }
    }
    // Returns null when filtered!
    return temp;
  }
}
```

This implementation has a problem, however. The getNextShape method not only returns a null value once the end of the list is reached, but also returns a null value for each Shape that is filtered. The Canvas class does not expect this behavior from a ShapeList and will incorrectly stop rendering when it tries to read a Shape subject to filtering. This example violates the Liskov Substitution Principle.

In this case, we can satisfy the principle by changing the getNextShape method so it will continue to traverse the shape list until it finds an unfiltered shape or until it reaches the end of the list.

The Liskov Substitution Principle also applies to methods. A method designed to recognize particular derivations of a superclass may not know how to handle a new derivation. The drawShape method in the Canvas class illustrates this problem. This method interrogates each incoming shape to determine its type in to dispatch it to the appropriate drawing routine. Developers would have to change the Canvas class and the drawShape method each time they wanted to add a new subclass of the Shape class.

This problem is solved by adding a drawSelf method to the Shape subclasses and replacing the shape-specific methods on the canvas with a set of primitive drawing operations that Shapes can use to draw themselves. Each subclass of Shape would override the drawSelf method to call the canvas drawing operations necessary to produce that particular shape. The drawShapes method on the canvas would no longer call drawShape to dispatch shapes to canvas routines, but would, instead, call the drawSelf method on each Shape subclass:

```
class Shape {
  ...
  public abstract void drawSelf(Canvas canvas);
  ...
}

class Circle extends Shape {
  ...
  public void drawSelf(Canvas canvas) {...}
  ...
}

class Canvas {
  ...
  public void drawShapes(ShapeList list) {
    Shape shape = list.getNextShape();

    // Use null to detect end of list
    while (shape != null) {
      // Tell the shape to draw itself
      shape.drawSelf(this);
      shape = list.getNextShape();
    }
  }

  // Define the operations the shapes will use
  public void drawLine(int x1,
                       int y1,
```

```
                        int x2,
                        int y2) {...}

    public void drawCircle(int x,
                            int y,
                            int radius) {...}
    ...
    }
```

### 71. Make all fields private.

> Out of sight, out of mind.—*Anonymous*

Doing so ensures the consistency of the member data because only the owning class may make changes to it. Access all member data through object methods. This minimizes coupling between objects, which enhances program maintainability.

### 72. Use polymorphism instead of `instanceof`.

Do not use `instanceof` to choose behavior depending upon an object's type. This forces you to modify the choice selection code every time the set of choice object types changes, leading to brittle code.

Instead, implement object-specific behavior in methods derived from a base class. This enables a client to interact with the base class abstraction without knowledge of the derived classes, allowing new classes to be introduced without the client's knowledge.

## Type Safety

### 73. Wrap general-purpose classes that operate on `java.lang.Object` to provide static type checking.

Ensure type safety by wrapping a general class that barters in `Object` types with one that casts objects to a specific type. The following code shows how to wrap a general-purpose queue to create a type-specific one:

```
public class Queue {
  public void enqueue(Object object) {...};
  public Object dequeue() {...};
}

public class OrderQueue {
  private Queue queue;

  public OrderQueue() {
    this.queue = new Queue();
  }

  public void enqueue(Order order) {
    this.queue.enqueue(order);
  }

  public Order dequeue() {
    return (Order)this.queue.dequeue();
  }
}
```

### 74. Encapsulate enumerations as classes.

Encapsulate enumerations as classes to provide type-safe comparisons of enumerator values:

```
public class Color {
  private static int count = 0;
  public static final Color RED =
    new Color(count++);
  public static final Color GREEN =
    new Color(count++);
  public static final Color BLUE =
    new Color(count++);
  private int value;

  private Color(int value) {
    this.value = value;
  }

  public boolean equals(Color other) {
    return this.value == other.value;
  }
```

```
  public static int Color.count() {
    return count;
  }
}

Color aColor = Color.RED;

if (anotherColor.equals(aColor)) {
  ...
}
```

# Statements and Expressions

## 75. *Replace repeated nontrivial expressions with equivalent methods.*

Write code once and only once. Factor out common functionality and repackage as a method or a class. This makes code easier to learn and understand. Changes are localized, so maintenance is easier and testing effort is reduced.

## 76. *Use block statements instead of expression statements in control flow constructs.*

The Java block statement provides a mechanism for treating any number of statements as a single compound statement. A block statement may be used anywhere a regular statement may be used, including the expression statement bodies of a Java control construct.

While the language enables you to use simple, nonblock statements as the body of these constructs, you should always use a block statement in these situations.

Block statements reduce the ambiguity that often arises when control constructs are nested, and they provide a mechanism for organizing the code for improved readability.

The following code fragment is confusing because the indentation makes it appear as though the else clause is associated with the first if statement, while the compiler will associate it with the second if statement. The Java language specification refers to this as the "dangling else problem." The use of block statements eliminates this problem:

```java
if (x >= 0)
  if (x > 0) positiveX();
else // Oops! Actually matches most recent if!
  negativeX();


if (x >= 0) {
  if (x > 0) positiveX();
}
else {
  negativeX(); // This is what we really wanted!
}
```

In the following example, the code on the top is more difficult to modify than the code on the bottom. This is because you cannot add another statement without changing the existing code structure. Because the code on the bottom already uses block statements, modifications are easier to make:

```java
for (int i = n; i >= 0; i--)
  for (int j = n; j >= 0; j--)
    f(i,j);
    // g(i,j) Cannot add here!


for (int i = n;i >= 0;i--) {
  for (int j = n;j >= 0;j--) {
    f(i,j);
    g(i,j); // Can add here!
  }
}
```

If a control statement has a single, trivial statement as its body, you may put the entire statement on a single line, but only if it improves readability. Treat this case as the exception rather than the norm.

## 77. *Clarify the order of operations with parentheses.*

The order of operations in a mathematical expression is not always obvious. Even if you are certain as to the order, you can safely assume others will not be so sure.

```
// Extraneous but useful parentheses.
int width = (( buffer * offset ) / pixelWidth )
            + gap;
```

## 78. *Always code a* `break` *statement in the last case of a switch statement.*

The following switch statement was coded with the assumption that no other cases would follow the Y case, so no break statement was required:

```
switch (...) {
  case X:
    ...
    break;
  case Y:
    ...
}
```

What if a new case is needed, however, and the person adding this case decides simply to add it after the last existing case, but fails to notice this case did not have a break statement? This person may inadvertently introduce a hard-to-detect "fall-through" error, as shown here:

```
switch (...) {
  case X:
    ...
    break;
  case Y:
    ...       // Oops! Unintended fall-through!
```

```
  case Z:
    ...
}
```

To prevent future problems, you should always code a break statement for the last case in the switch statement, even if it is the default case:

```
switch (...) {
  case X:
    ...
    break;
  case Y:
    ...
    break; // OK! No more fall-through!
  case Z:
    ...
    break;
  default:
    ... // Complain about value!
    break;
}
```

Do not forget to add a "fall-through" comment in those cases that really do "fall-through." See Rule #65.

## 79. Use **equals()**, *not* ==, *to test for equality of objects.*

Many C++ programmers make this mistake when dealing with Java dates and strings:

```
Date today = new Date();
while (date != today) {
  ...
}

String name;
...
if (name == "Bob") {
  hiBob();
}
```

In Java, the "!=" and "==" operators compare object identities, not object values. You must use the equals method to compare the actual strings:

```java
Date today = new Date();
while (!date.equals(today)) {
  ...
}

String name;
...
if ("Bob".equals(name)) {
  hiBob();
}
```

Note, unlike the expression name.equals("Bob"), the expression "Bob".equals(name) does not throw an exception if name is null.

## Construction

### 80. Always construct objects in a valid state.

Never allow an invalid object to be constructed. If an object must be constructed in an invalid state and then must undergo further initialization before it becomes valid, use a static method that coordinates the multistage construction. The construction method should construct the object so that when the method completes, the new object is in a valid state. Hide any constructors that do not construct valid instances by making them protected or private.

### 81. Do not call nonfinal methods from within a constructor.

Subclasses may override nonfinal methods and Java will dispatch a call to such a method according to the actual type of the constructed object—before executing the derived class constructors. This means when the constructor invokes the derived method, the derived class may be in an invalid state. To prevent this, call only final methods from the constructor.

## 82. Use nested constructors to eliminate redundant code.

To avoid writing redundant constructor code, call lower-level constructors from higher-level constructors.

This code implements the same low-level initialization in two different places:

```
class Account {
  String name;
  double balance;
  final static double DEFAULT_BALANCE = 0.0d;

  Account(String name, double balance) {
    this.name = name;
    this.balance = balance;
  }

  Account(String name) {
    this.name = name;
    this.balance = DEFAULT_BALANCE;
  }
}
```

This code implements the low-level initialization in one place only:

```
class Account {
  String name;
  double balance;
  final static double DEFAULT_BALANCE = 0.0d;

  Account(String name, double balance) {
    this.name = name;
    this.balance = balance;
  }
```

```
   Account(String name) {
     this(name, DEFAULT_BALANCE);
   }
}
```

This approach is also helpful if you are using assertions, as it typically reduces the number of places a given constructor argument appears, thus reducing the number of places the validity of that argument is checked.

## Exception Handling

*83. Use unchecked, run-time exceptions to report serious unexpected errors that may indicate an error in the program's logic.*

Catching and handling run-time exceptions is possible, however, they are usually of such a severe nature that program termination is imminent. Run-time exceptions are usually thrown because of programming errors, such as failed assertions, using an out-of-bound index, dividing by zero, or referencing a null pointer.

*84. Use checked exceptions to report errors that may occur, however rarely, under normal program operation.*

Checked exceptions indicate a serious problem that should not occur under normal conditions. The caller must catch this exception. Depending upon the application, a program may be able to recover from a checked exception; that is, it doesn't indicate a fundamental flaw in the program's logic.

### 85. *Use return codes to report expected state changes.*

For expected state changes, use a return code, sentinel, or special method that returns a status. This makes code more readable and the flow of control straightforward. For example, in the course of reading from a file, it is expected the end of the file will be reached at some point.

### 86. *Only convert exceptions to add information.*

Retain all exception information; never discard lower-level explanations:

```
try {
  for(int i = v.size(); --i >= 0;) {
    ostream.println(v.elementAt(i));
  }
}
catch (ArrayOutOfBounds e) {
  // should never get here
  throw new UnexpectedExceptionError(e);
}
```

### 87. *Do not silently absorb a run-time or error exception.*

Breaking this rule makes code hard to debug because information is lost:

```
try {
  for(int i = v.size(); --i >- 0;) {
    ostream.println(v.elementAt(i));
  }
}
catch (ArrayOutOfBounds e) {
  // Oops! We should never get here...
  // ... but if we do, nobody will ever know!
}
```

Even if you have coded a catch block simply to catch an exception you do not expect to occur, at least print a "stack trace." You never know when something "impossible" might occur within your software:

```
try {
  for (int i=v.size(); --i>=0;) {
    ostream.println(v.elementAt(i));
  }
}
catch (ArrayOutOfBounds e) {
  // Oops! Should never get here...
  // But print a stack trace just in case...
  e.printStackTrace();
}
```

## 88. Use a `finally` block to release resources.

Once a try-block is entered, any corresponding `finally` block is guaranteed to be executed. This makes the `finally` block a good place to release any resources acquired prior to entering or within the try-block.

In this first example, if an exception or return occurs following the creation of the output stream, the function will exit without closing and flushing the stream:

```
public void logSomeStuff() {
  OutputStream log = new FileOutputStream("log");
  ...
  // could get exception here!
  ...
  log.close();
}
```

In this example, we use a `finally` block to ensure the stream is always closed when the thread of execution exits the try-block. This is done even if the thread exits the block because an exception has been thrown or a return statement was executed:

```
OutputStream log = null;
try {
  log = new FileOutputStream("log");
}
finally {
  if (log != null) {
    log.close();
  }
}
```

# Assertions

## 89. *Program by contract.*

Consider each method a contract between the caller and the callee. The contract states[28] the caller must abide by the "preconditions" of a method and the method, in turn, must return results that satisfy the "postconditions" associated with that method.

Abiding by the preconditions of a method usually means passing parameters as the method expects them; it may also mean calling a set of methods in the correct order. To abide by the postconditions of the method, the method must correctly complete the work it was called upon to perform and it must leave the object in a consistent state.

Check preconditions and postconditions by assertion (see Rule #92) in any appropriate public methods. Check preconditions at the beginning of a method, before any other code is executed, and check postconditions at the end of a method before the method returns.

Derived class methods that override base class methods must preserve the pre- and postconditions of the base class method. To ensure this, use the template method design pattern.[29]

Make each public method final and create a parallel nonfinal protected method that implements the body of the function. The public final method tests preconditions, calls the associated protected method, and then tests postconditions. A deriving class may override public behavior in the base class by overriding the nonfinal protected method associated with each public final method:

```
class LinkedList {
  public final synchronized void
    prepend(Object object) {

    // Test pre-condition
    if (Assert.ENABLED)
      Assert.isTrue(object != null);
    doPrepend(object);
    // Test post-condition
    if (Assert.ENABLED)
      Assert.isTrue(first() == object);
  }

  protected void doPrepend(Object object) {
    Node node = new Node(object);
    if (this.head == null)
      this.head = node;
    else {
      node.next = this.head;
      this.head = node;
    }
  }
}
```

This technique also works to ensure that a method will remain synchronized, even when overridden. A derived class may violate the synchronization semantics of a base class by overriding a synchronized method with an unsynchronized version of the method—derived class methods do not inherit the synchronized qualifier. A superclass can guarantee synchronization by providing a public final synchronized method that calls the nonfinal method.

### 90. Use dead code elimination to implement assertions.

An *assertion* is an expression you, the programmer, insist must hold true for a piece of code to operate correctly. Assertions are used in code to ensure basic coding assumptions are not violated. If an assertion evaluates to false, the code is flawed.

Use assertions liberally throughout code to test the basic premises upon which the code was built. Assertions take time to execute, though, and we usually want to remove them from the released code. For this, we can take advantage of dead code elimination.

*Dead code elimination* occurs when a Java compiler eliminates unreachable code. For example, when a compiler sees the following piece of code, it knows the variable FALSE will always evaluate to false, as it is a static final variable. This allows the compiler to eliminate the block of code following the if expression, as the compiler knows it can never evaluate to true:

```
class DeadCode {
  static final boolean FALSE = false;
  public void example() {
    if (FALSE) {
      System.out.println("Never to be seen.");
    }
  }
}
```

Using what we know about dead code elimination, we can write an assertion class that will enable us to choose when to include assertions in the compiler-generated code:

```
public class Assert {
  public static final boolean ENABLED=true;
  public static final void
    isTrue(boolean assertion) {
    if (Assert.ENABLED && !assertion)
```

```
    throw new
      RuntimeException("Assertion Failed");
  }
}
...
if (Assert.ENABLED) Assert.isTrue(a > b);
...
```

To turn assertions off, set the ENABLED variable in the Assert class to false.

 Failed assertions indicate an error in program logic, either in the use of a method or in the implementation of that method. For this reason, report assertion failures by throwing an unchecked exception such as RuntimeException or some derivation thereof.

### 91. Use assertions to catch logic errors in your code.

An assertion is a Boolean expression that must hold true for a program to operate correctly. Use assertions to validate the assumptions made by a program.

### 92. Use assertions to test pre- and postconditions of a method.

A method's *preconditions* are those conditions required for the method's proper execution. For example, a precondition may test the validity of the parameters passed to the method or test that the object is in a valid state.

*Postcondition* assertions execute at the completion of a method to verify the object is still in a valid state and the return values of the method are reasonable.

# Concurrency

*Concurrency* exists when two or more threads make progress, executing instructions at the same time. A single processor system can support concurrency by switching execution between two or more threads. A multiprocessor system can support parallel concurrency by executing a separate thread on each processor. A class is *multithread-hot* or *MT-hot* if it creates additional threads to accomplish its task.

Many applications can benefit from the use of concurrency in their implementation. In a concurrent model of execution, an application is divided into two or more processes or threads, each executing in its own sequence of statements or instructions. An application may consist of one or more processes and a process may consist of one or more threads. Execution may be distributed on two or more machines in a network, two or more processors in a single machine, or interleaved on a single processor.

The separately executing processes or threads must generally compete for access to shared resources and data, and must cooperate to accomplish their overall task.

Concurrent application development is a complicated task. Designing a concurrent application involves determining the necessary number of processes or threads, their particular responsibilities, and the methods by which they will interact. It also involves determining the good, legal, or invariant program states and the bad or illegal program states. The critical problem is to find and implement a solution that maintains or guarantees good program states while prohibiting bad program states, even in those situations where two or more threads may be acting on the same resource.

In a concurrent environment, a programmer maintains desirable program states by limiting or negotiating access to shared resources using synchronization. The principle role of synchronization is to prevent undesirable or unanticipated interference between simultaneously executing instruction sequences.

### 93. Use threads only where appropriate.

Threads are not a "silver bullet" for improving application performance. An application not suited for multithreading may run slower following the introduction of multiple threads because of the overhead required to switch between threads.

Before you introduce threads into your application, determine whether it can benefit from their use. Use threads if your application needs:[30]

- To react to many events simultaneously.
  Examples: An Internet browser or server.

- To provide a high level of responsiveness.
  Example: A user-interface implementation that can continue to respond to user actions even while the application is performing other computations.

- To take advantage of machines with multiple processors.
  Example: An application targeted for particular machine architectures.

## Synchronization

*Synchronization* describes the set of mechanisms or processes for preventing undesirable interleaving of operations or interference between concurrent threads. A programmer may choose between one of two synchronization techniques: *mutual exclusion* or *condition synchronization*.

*Mutual exclusion* involves combining fine-grained *atomic* actions into coarse-grained actions and arranging to make these composite actions atomic.

*Condition synchronization* describes a process or mechanism that delays the execution of a thread until the program satisfies some predicate or condition.

A thread that is no longer executing because it is delayed or waiting on some synchronization mechanism is *blocked*. Once *unblocked*, *awakened*, or *notified*, a thread becomes *runnable* and eligible for further execution.

Two basic uses exist for thread synchronization: to protect the integrity of shared data and to communicate changes efficiently in program state between cooperating threads.

Java supports both mutual exclusion and condition synchronization via a mechanism provided by the `Object` class.

### 94. Avoid synchronization.

Synchronization is expensive. It takes time to acquire and release the synchronization objects necessary to synchronize a section of code. Moreover, synchronization serializes access to an object, minimizing concurrency. Think before you synchronize and only synchronize when it's truly necessary.

Do not arbitrarily synchronize every public method. Before  synchronizing a method, consider whether it accesses shared and nonsynchronized states. If it does not—if the method only operates on its local variables, parameters, or synchronized objects—then synchronization is not required.

Do not synchronize classes that provide fundamental data types or structures. Let the users of the object determine whether synchronization is necessary. Users may always synchronize the object externally under the jurisdiction of a separate lock object.

### 95. Use synchronized wrappers to provide synchronized interfaces.

Use synchronized wrappers to provide synchronized versions of classes. *Synchronized wrappers* provide the same interface as the original class, but its methods are synchronized. A static method of the wrapped class provides access to the synchronized wrapper. The following example demonstrates a stack, which has a default, nonsynchronized interface and a synchronized interface provided by a wrapper class:

```java
public class Stack {
  public void push(Object o) {...};
  public Object pop() {...};
  public static Stack createSynchronizedStack() {
    return new SynchronizedStack();
  }
}

class SynchronizedStack extends Stack {

  public synchronized void push(Object o) {
    super.push(o);
  }

  public synchronized Object pop() {
    return super.pop();
  }
}
```

### 96. Do not synchronize an entire method if the method contains significant operations that do not need synchronization.

To maximize concurrency in a program, we must minimize the frequency and duration of lock acquisition. A thread entering a synchronized method or block attempts to acquire a lock. Only one thread at a time may acquire ownership of a lock, so a lock may be used to serialize access to code or a program state. When a thread has finished executing in the synchronized section of code, it releases the lock so others threads may attempt to acquire ownership.

A method annotated with the synchronized keyword acquires a lock on the associated object at the beginning of the method and holds that lock until the end of the method. As is often the case, however, only a few operations within a method may require synchronization. In these situations, the method-level synchronization can be much too coarse.

The alternative to method-level synchronization is to use the synchronized block statement:

```
protected void processRequest () {
  Request request = getNextRequest();
  RequestId id = request.getId();
  synchronize(this) {
    RequestHandler handler =
      this.handlerMap.get(id);
  }
  handler.handle(request);
}
```

### 97. Avoid unnecessary synchronization when reading or writing instance variables.

The Java language guarantees read-and-write actions are atomic for object references and all primitives, except for type long and type double. We can, therefore, avoid the use of synchronization when reading or writing atomic data. Be careful, though. If the value of an atomic variable is dependent on or related to the other variables, then synchronization is necessary.

In this example, the assignment of x and y must be synchronized together because they are interdependent values:

```
public void synchronized setCenter(int x, int y) {
    this.x = x;
    this.y = y;
}
```

The following example does not require synchronization because it uses an atomic assignment of an object reference:

```
public void setCenter(Point p) {
    this.point = (Point)p.clone();
}
```

## 98. Consider using `notify()` instead of `notifyAll()`.

The `notify()` method of `java.lang.Object` awakens a single thread waiting on a condition, while `notifyAll()` awakens all threads waiting on the condition. If possible, use `notify()` instead of `notifyAll()` because `notify()` is more efficient.

Use `notify()` when threads are waiting on a single condition and when only a single waiting thread may proceed at a time. For example, if the `notify()` signals that an item has been written to a queue, only one thread will be able to read the item from the queue. In this case, waking up more than one thread is wasteful.

Use `notifyAll()` when threads may wait on more than one condition or if it is possible for more than one thread to proceed in response to a signal.

## 99. Use the double-check pattern for synchronized initialization.

Use the double-check pattern[31] in situations where synchronization is required during initialization, but not after it.

In the following code, the instance variable `log` needs to be initialized, but only if it is `null`. To prevent two threads from trying to initialize the field simultaneously, the function getLog() is declared synchronized:

```
synchronized Log getLog() {
  if (this.log==null) {
    this.log = new Log();
  }
  return this.log;
}
```

This code also protects against simultaneous initialization, but it uses the double-check pattern to avoid synchronization except during initialization:

```
Log getLog() {
  if (this.log==null) {
    synchronized (this) {
      if (this.log==null) {
        this.log = new Log();
      }
    }
  }
  return this.log;
}
```

# Efficiency

### 100. Use lazy initialization.

Do not build something until you need it. If an object may not be needed during the normal course of program execution, then do not build the object until it is required.

Use an accessor method to gain access to the object. All users of that object, including within the same class, must use the accessor to get a reference to the object:

```
class PersonalFinance {
  LoanRateCalculator loanCalculator = null;

  LoanRateCalculator getLoanCalculator() {
    if (this.loanCalculator == null)
```

```
      this.loanCalculator =
        new LoanRateCalculator();
      return this.loanCalculator;
  }
}
```

### 101. *Avoid creating unnecessary objects.*

This is especially important if the new objects have short life
spans or are constructed, but never referenced. This not only
wastes execution time to create the object, but it also uses
time during garbage collection.

Redundant initialization, as illustrated in the following code,
is quite common, and wasteful:

```
Color getTextColor() {
  Color c = new Color(...);
  if (this.state < 2) {
    c = new Color(...);
  }
  return c;
}
```

Avoid creating an object until you know what you want:

```
Color getTextColor() {
  Color c = null;
  if (this.state < 2) {
    c = new Color(...);
  } else {
    c = new Color(...);
  }
  return c;
}
```

### 102. *Reinitialize and reuse objects to avoid new object construction.*

Cache and reuse frequently created objects that have limited
life spans.

Use accessor methods instead of constructors to reinitialize the object.

Take care to choose an implementation that does not need to create its own objects to manage the objects being cached. This would defeat the purpose!

Use a factory implementation to encapsulate mechanisms for caching and reusing objects. To manage these mechanisms properly, you must return objects obtained from an object factory back to the same factory. This means the association between an object and its factory must be maintained somewhere:

- In the class—a single static factory is associated with the class of the object, and that factory manages all objects of that class.

- In the object—the object maintains a reference to the factory that manages it.

- In the owner of the object—an "owner" of an object maintains a reference to the factory from which the object obtained

## 103. Leave optimization for last.

**First Rule of Optimization:**
Don't do it.
**Second Rule of Optimization (For experts only):**
Don't do it yet.
—*Michael Jackson,*
*Michael Jackson Systems Ltd.*

Do not waste time optimizing code until you are sure you need to do it.

Remember the 80–20 rule[32]—20 percent of the code in a system uses 80 percent of the resources (on average). If you are going to optimize, make sure it falls within the 20 percent portion.

24 Barbara Liskov, and John Guttag. *Abstraction and Specification in Program Development.* (New York: McGraw–Hill, 1986).

25 Robert Martin. "Engineering Notebook," *C++ Report,* Vol. 8, No. 3 (Mar 1996). Accessed online at http://www.objectmentor.com/publications/lsp.pdf, Aug 1999.

26 Barbara Liskov originally described this concept with the following statement: "If for each object O1 of type S there is an object O2 of type T such that for all programs P defined in terms of T, the behavior of P is unchanged when O1 is substituted for O2 then S is a subtype of T."

27 Robert Martin. "Engineering Notebook: The Open–Closed Principle," *C++ Report,* Vol. 8, No. 1 (Jan 1996). Accessed online at http://www.objectmentor.com/publications/ocp.pdf, Aug 1999.

28 Bertrand Meyer. *Object-Oriented Software Construction.*

29 Erich Gamma et al. *Design Patterns: Elements of Reusable Object-Oriented Software.* (Reading, Massachusetts: Addison–Wesley, 1995). pp. 325–330.

30 Doug Lea. *Concurrent Programming in Java™: Design Principles and Patterns.* (Reading, Massachusetts: Addison–Wesley, 1997). pp. 1–2.

31 Douglas C. Schmidt and Tim Harrison. *Pattern Languages of Program Design.* (Reading, Massachusetts: Addison–Wesley, 1997).

32 Steve McConnell. *Code Complete.* (Redmond, Washington: Microsoft Press, 1993). pp. 681–682.

# 6.

# Packaging
# Conventions

THIS SECTION contains guidelines for creating packages. See Rules #15–17 for conventions related to package naming.

**104. *Place types that are commonly used, changed, and released together, or mutually dependent on each other, into the same package.***

This rule encompasses several related package design principles[33]:

> **The Common Reuse Principle**
> A package consists of classes you reuse together.
> If you use one of the classes in the package, you use all of them.

Place classes and interfaces you usually use together into the same package. Such classes are so closely coupled you cannot use one class without usually using the other. Some examples of closely related types include

- Containers and iterators.
- Database tables, rows, and columns.
- Calendars, dates, and times.
- Points, lines, and polygons.

### The Common Closure Principle
A package consists of classes, all closed against the same kind of changes. A change that affects the package affects all the classes in that package.

Combine classes that are likely to change at the same time, for the same reasons, into a single package. If two classes are so closely related that changing one of them usually involves changing the other, then place them in the same package.

### The Reuse/Release Equivalence Principle
The unit of reuse is the unit of release. Effective reuse requires tracking of releases from a change control system. The package is the effective unit of reuse and release.

Treating individual classes as a unit of release is not very practical. A typical application may consist of tens of hundreds of classes, so releasing code on a class-by-class basis will dramatically complicate the integration and testing process, and dramatically increase the overall rate of change within the software.

A package provides a much more convenient mechanism for releasing several classes and interfaces. Each class or interface within a package may undergo several independent revisions between releases, but a package release captures only the latest version of each class and interface. Use packages as the primary unit of release and distribution.

### The Acyclic Dependencies Principle
The dependency structure between packages must be a directed acyclic graph; there must be no cycles in the dependency structure.

If two packages directly or indirectly depend on each other, you cannot independently release one without releasing the other because changes in one package will often force changes in the other. Such cyclic dependencies dramatically increase the fragility of a system and can eliminate any reduction in schedule realized by assigning the development of each package to separate developers or teams.

Take steps to eliminate cyclic dependencies, either by combining the mutually dependent packages or by introducing a new package of abstractions that both packages can depend on instead of each other.

## 105. Isolate volatile classes and interfaces in separate packages.

Avoid placing volatile classes and interfaces in the same package with stable classes and interfaces. If you use packages as your principle unit of release and distribution, users can gain access to the latest changes in the volatile classes and interfaces only if you re-release the entire package. Each time you release the package, your users must absorb the cost of reintegrating and retesting against all the classes in the package, although many may not have changed.

Separate volatile classes from stable classes to reduce the code footprint affected by new releases of code, thereby reducing the impact on users of that code.

## 106. Avoid making packages that are difficult to change dependent on packages that are easy to change.

This rule derives from the following design principle[34]:

**The Stable Dependencies Principle**
The dependencies between packages should be oriented in the direction of increasing stability. A package should only depend on packages more stable than it is.

If a package containing difficult-to-change types is dependent on a package that contains easy, or likely to change, types, then the dependent package effectively acts to impede change in the volatile package.

In a software system, especially one that is incrementally developed, some packages will always remain somewhat volatile. The developers of such a system must feel free to modify and extend these volatile packages to complete the implementation of the system and must be able to do so without worrying too much about downstream effects.

Do not create a package that depends on less stable packages. If necessary, create new abstractions that can be used to invert the relationship between the stable code and the unstable code.

### 107. Maximize abstraction to maximize stability.

This rule derives from the following design principle[35]:

**The Stable Abstractions Principle**
The stability exhibited by a package is directly proportional to its level of abstraction. The more abstract a package is, the more stable it tends to be. The more concrete a package is, the more unstable it tends to be.

Use stable abstractions to create stable packages. Capture high-level, stable concepts in abstract classes and interfaces, and provide implementations using concrete classes. Separate abstract classes and interfaces from the concrete classes to form stable and unstable packages. This ensures the derived classes in the unstable packages depend on the abstract base classes and interfaces in the stable packages.

## 108. Capture high-level design and architecture as stable abstractions organized into stable packages.

To plan and manage a software development effort successfully, the top-level design must stabilize quickly and remain that way. No development manager can hope to accurately plan, estimate, schedule, and allocate resources if the architecture of the system continues to change.

Once the design of the high-level architecture is complete, use packages to separate the stable parts of the design from the volatile implementation. Create packages to capture the high-level abstractions of the design. Place the detailed implementation of those abstractions into separate packages that depend on the high-level abstract packages.

---

33 Robert Martin. "Engineering Notebook: Granularity," *C++ Report*, Vol. 8, No. 10 (Nov 1996), pp. 57-62. Accessed online at http://www.objectmentor.com/publications/granularity.pdf, Aug 1999.

34 Robert Martin. "Engineering Notebook: Stability," *C++ Report*, Vol. 9, No. 2 (Feb 1997). Accessed online at http://www.objectmentor.com/publications/stability.pdf, Aug 1999.

35 Ibid.

# Summary

1. *Adhere to the style of the original.*

2. *Adhere to the Principle of Least Astonishment.*

3. *Do it right the first time.*

4. *Document any deviations.*

5. *Indent nested code.*

6. *Break up long lines.*

7. *Include white space.*

8. *Do not use "hard" tabs.*

9. *Use meaningful names.*

10. *Use familiar names.*

11. *Question excessively long names.*

12. *Join the vowel generation.*

13. *Capitalize only the first letter in acronyms.*

14. *Do not use names that differ only in case.*

15. *Use the reversed, lowercase form of your organization's Internet domain name as the root qualifier for your package names.*

16. *Use a single, lowercase word as the root name of each package.*

17. *Use the same name for a new version of a package, but only if that new version is still* binary compatible *with the previous version, otherwise, use a new name.*

18. *Capitalize the first letter of each word that appears in a class or interface name.*

19. *Use nouns when naming classes.*

20. *Pluralize the names of classes that group related attributes, static services, or constants.*

21. *Use nouns or adjectives when naming interfaces.*

22. *Use lowercase for the first word and capitalize only the first letter of each subsequent word that appears in a method name.*

23. *Use verbs when naming methods.*

24. *Follow the JavaBeans™ conventions for naming property accessor methods.*

25. Use lowercase for the first word and capitalize only the first letter of each subsequent word that appears in a variable name.

26. Use nouns to name fields.

27. Pluralize the names of collection references.

28. Establish and use a set of standard names for trivial "throwaway" variables.

29. Qualify field variables with "`this`" to distinguish them from local variables.

30. When a constructor or "set" method assigns a parameter to a field, give that parameter the same name as the field.

31. Use uppercase letters for each word and separate each pair of words with an underscore when naming constants.

32. Write documentation for those who must use your code and those who must maintain it.

33. Keep comments and code in sync.

34. Use the active voice and omit needless words.

35. Use documentation comments to describe the programming interface.

36. *Use standard comments to hide code without removing it.*

37. *Use one-line comments to explain implementation details.*

38. *Describe the programming interface before you write the code.*

39. *Document public, protected, package, and private members.*

40. *Provide a summary description and overview for each package.*

41. *Provide a summary description and overview for each application or group of packages.*

42. *Use a single consistent format and organization for all documentation comments.*

43. *Wrap keywords, identifiers, and constants with* `<code>...</code>` *tags.*

44. *Wrap code with* `<pre>...</pre>` *tags.*

45. *Consider marking the first occurrence of an identifier with a* `{@link}` *tag.*

46. *Establish and use a fixed ordering for Javadoc tags.*

47. *Write in the third-person narrative form.*

48. *Write summary descriptions that stand alone.*

49. *Omit the subject in summary descriptions of actions or services.*

50. *Omit the subject and the verb in summary descriptions of things.*

51. *Use "this" rather than "the" when referring to instances of the current class.*

52. *Do not add parentheses to a method or constructor name unless you want to specify a particular signature.*

53. *Provide a summary description for each class, interface, field, and method.*

54. *Fully describe the signature of each method.*

55. *Include examples.*

56. *Document preconditions, postconditions, and invariant conditions.*

57. *Document known defects and deficiencies.*

58. *Document synchronization semantics.*

59. *Add internal comments only if they will aid others in understanding your code.*

60. *Describe* why *the code is doing what it does, not* what *the code is doing.*

61. *Avoid the use of end-line comments.*

62. *Explain local variable declarations with an end-line comment.*

63. *Establish and use a set of keywords to flag unresolved issues.*

64. *Label closing braces in highly nested control structures.*

65. *Add a "fall-through" comment between two* `case` *labels, if no* `break` *statement separates those labels.*

66. *Label empty statements.*

67. *Consider declaring classes representing fundamental data types as* `final`.

68. *Build concrete types from native types and other concrete types.*

69. *Define small classes and small methods.*

70. *Define subclasses so they may be used anywhere their superclasses may be used.*

71. *Make all fields private.*

72. *Use polymorphism instead of* `instanceof`.

73. *Wrap general-purpose classes that operate on* `java.lang.Object` *to provide static type checking.*

74. *Encapsulate enumerations as classes.*

75. *Replace repeated nontrivial expressions with equivalent methods.*

76. *Use block statements instead of expression statements in control flow constructs.*

77. *Clarify the order of operations with parentheses.*

78. *Always code a* `break` *statement in the last case of a switch statement.*

79. *Use* `equals()`, *not* `==`, *to test for equality of objects.*

80. *Always construct objects in a valid state.*

81. *Do not call nonfinal methods from within a constructor.*

82. *Use nested constructors to eliminate redundant code.*

83. *Use unchecked, run-time exceptions to report serious unexpected errors that may indicate an error in the program's logic.*

84. *Use checked exceptions to report errors that may occur, however rarely, under normal program operation.*

85. *Use return codes to report expected state changes.*

86. *Only convert exceptions to add information.*

87. *Do not silently absorb a run-time or error exception.*

88. *Use a* `finally` *block to release resources.*

89. *Program by contract.*

90. *Use dead code elimination to implement assertions.*

91. *Use assertions to catch logic errors in your code.*

92. *Use assertions to test pre- and postconditions of a method.*

93. *Use threads only where appropriate.*

94. *Avoid synchronization.*

95. *Use synchronized wrappers to provide synchronized interfaces.*

96. *Do not synchronize an entire method if the method contains significant operations that do not need synchronization.*

97. *Avoid unnecessary synchronization when reading or writing instance variables.*

98. *Consider using* `notify()` *instead of* `notifyAll()`.

99. *Use the double-check pattern for synchronized initialization.*

100. *Use lazy initialization.*

101. *Avoid creating unnecessary objects.*

102. *Reinitialize and reuse objects to avoid new object construction.*

103. *Leave optimization for last.*

104. *Place types that are commonly used, changed, and released together, or mutually dependent on each other, into the same package.*

105. *Isolate volatile classes and interfaces in separate packages.*

106. *Avoid making packages that are difficult to change dependent on packages that are easy to change.*

107. *Maximize abstraction to maximize stability.*

108. *Capture high-level design and architecture as stable abstractions organized into stable packages.*

# Glossary

**abstract class**

A class that exists only as a superclass of another class and can never be directly instantiated. In Java, an abstract class contains or inherits one or more abstract methods or includes the abstract keyword in its definition.

**abstract method**

A method that has no implementation.

**abstract data type**

Defines a type that may have many implementations. Abstract data types include things like stacks, queues, and trees.

**abstract type**

Defines the type for a set of objects, where each object must also belong to a set of objects that conform to a known subtype of the abstract type. An abstract type may have one or more implementations.

**abstraction**

The process and result of extracting the common or general characteristics from a set of similar entities.

**accessor**

A method that sets or gets the value of an object property or attribute.

**active object**

An object that possesses its own thread of control.

**acyclic dependency**
A dependency relationship where one entity has a direct or indirect dependency on a second entity, but the second entity has no direct or indirect dependency on the first.

**aggregation**
An association representing a whole–part containment relationship.

**architecture**
A description of the organization and structure of a software system.

**argument**
Data item specified as a parameter in a method call.

**assertion**
A statement about the truth of a logical expression.

**attribute**
A named characteristic or property of a type, class, or object.

**behavior**
The activities and effects produced by an object in response to an event.

**binary compatible**
A situation where one version of a software component may be directly and transparently substituted for another version of that component without recompiling the component's clients.

**block statement**
> The Java language construct that combines one or more statement expressions into a single compound statement, by enclosing them in curly braces "{ ... }".

**Boolean**
> An enumerated type whose values are *true* and *false*.

**built-in type**
> A data type defined as part of the language. The built-in or *native* types defined by Java include the primitive types `boolean`, `byte`, `char`, `double`, `float`, `int`, `long`, `short`, and `void`, and the various classes and interfaces defined in the standard Java API, such as `Object`, `String`, `Thread`, and so forth.

**checked exception**
> Any exception that is not derived from `java.lang.RuntimeException` or `java.lang.Error`, or that appears in the `throws` clause of a method. A method that throws, or is a recipient of, a checked exception must handle the exception internally or otherwise declare the exception in its own `throws` clause.

**class**
> A set of objects that share the same attributes and behavior.

**class hierarchy**
> A set of classes associated by inheritance relationships.

**client**
> An entity that requests a service from another entity.

**cohesion**
> The degree to which two or more entities belong together or relate to each other.

**component**
> A physical and discrete software entity that conforms to a set of interfaces.

**composition**
> A form of aggregation where an object is composed of other objects.

**concrete class**
> A completely specified class that may be directly instantiated. A concrete class defines a specific implementation for an abstract class or type.

**concrete type**
> A type that may be directly instantiated. A concrete type may refine or extend an abstract type.

**concurrency**
> The degree by which two or more activities occur or make progress at the same time.

**constraint**
> A restriction on the value or behavior of an entity.

**constructor**
> A special method that initializes a new instance of a class.

**container**
> An object whose purpose is to contain and manipulate other objects.

**contract**

A clear description of the responsibilities and constraints that apply between a client and a type, class, or method.

**coupling**

The degree to which two or more entities are dependent on each other.

**critical section**

A block of code that allows only one thread at a time to enter and execute the instructions within that block. Any threads attempting to enter a critical section while another thread is already executing within that section are blocked until the original thread exits.

**cyclic dependency**

A dependency relationship where one entity has a direct or indirect dependency on a second entity and the second entity also has a direct or indirect dependency on the first.

**data type**

A primitive or built-in type that represents pure data and has no distinct identity as an object.

**delegation**

The act of passing a message, and responsibility, from one object to a second object to elicit a desired response.

**dependency**

A relationship where the semantic characteristics of one entity rely upon and constrain the semantic characteristics of another entity.

**derivation**
> The process of defining a new type or class by specializing or extending the behavior and attributes of an existing type or class.

**documentation comment**
> A comment that begins with a "/**" and ends with "*/", and contains a description and special tags that are parsed by the Javadoc utility to produce documentation.

**domain**
> An area of expertise, knowledge, or activity.

**encapsulation**
> The degree to which an appropriate mechanism is used to hide the internal data, structure, and implementation of an object or other entity.

**enumeration**
> A type that defines a list of named values that make up the allowable range for values of that type.

**factor**
> The act of reorganizing one or more types or classes by extracting responsibilities from existing classes and synthesizing new classes to handle these responsibilities.

**field**
> An instance variable or data member of an object.

**fundamental data type**
> A type that typically requires only one implementation and is commonly used to construct other, more useful types. Dates, complex numbers, linked-lists, and vectors are examples of common fundamental data types.

**generalization**

The process of extracting the common or general characteristics from a set of similar entities to create a new entity that possesses these common characteristics.

**implementation**

The concrete realization of a contract defined by a type, abstract class, or interface. The actual code.

**implementation class**

A concrete class that provides an implementation for a type, abstract class, or interface.

**implementation inheritance**

The action or mechanism by which a subclass inherits the implementation and interface from one or more parent classes.

**inheritance**

The mechanism by which more specialized entities acquire or incorporate the responsibilities or implementation of more generalized entities.

**inner-class**

A class defined within the scope of another class.

**instance**

The result of instantiating a class—the concrete representation of an object.

**instantiation**

The action or mechanism by which a type or class is reified to create an actual object. The act of allocating and initializing an object from a class.

**interface**

The methods exposed by a type, class, or object. Also a set of operations that define an abstract service.

**interface inheritance**

The action or mechanism by which a subtype or subinterface inherits the interface from one or more parent types or interfaces.

**invariant**

An expression that describes the well-defined, legal states of an object.

**keyword**

A language construct. The keywords of the Java language include:

| | | |
|---|---|---|
| abstract | finally | public |
| boolean | float | return |
| break | for | short |
| byte | [goto] | static |
| case | if | super |
| catch | implements | switch |
| char | import | synchronized |
| class | instanceof | this |
| [const] | int | throw |
| continue | interface | throws |
| default | long | transient |
| do | native | try |
| double | new | void |
| else | package | volatile |
| extends | private | while |
| final | protected | |

Bracketed keywords are reserved but not used.

**lazy initialization**
> When an implementation delays the initialization of a data value until the first use or access of the data value.

**local variable**
> A variable that is automatically allocated and initialized on the call "stack." Includes variables bound as function arguments.

**method**
> The implementation of an operation. An operation defined by an interface or class.

**multiple inheritance**
> Inheritance relationship where a subtype inherits from two or more supertypes. Java supports multiple inheritance by allowing an interface to extend multiple interfaces.

**mutex**
> A synchronization mechanism used to provide mutually exclusive access to a resource.

**native type**
> A data type defined as part of the language. The native or *built-in* types defined by Java include the *primitive* types `boolean`, `byte`, `char`, `double`, `float`, `int`, `long`, `short`, and `void`, and the various classes and interfaces defined in the standard Java API, such as `Object`, `String`, and `Thread`.

**object**
> The result of instantiating a class. An entity with state, behavior, and identity.

**operation**
A service that may be requested from an object to effect behavior. Alternatively viewed as a message sent from a client to an object.

**package**
A mechanism organizing and naming a collection of related classes.

**package access**
The default access-control characteristic applied to interfaces, classes, and class members. Class members with package access are accessible only to code within the same package and are heritable by subclasses in the same package. Classes and interfaces with package access are not visible to code outside the package. They are only accessible and extendable by classes and interfaces in the same package.

**parameter**
A variable that is bound to an argument value passed into a method.

**polymorphic**
A trait or characteristic of an object whereby that object can appear as several different types at the same time.

**polymorphism**
The concept or mechanism by which objects of different types inherit the responsibility for implementing the same operation, but respond differently to the invocation of that operation.

**postcondition**
A constraint or assertion that must hold true following the completion of an operation.

**precondition**
A constraint or assertion that must hold true at the start of an operation.

**primitive type**
A basic language type that represents a pure value and has no distinct identity as an object. The primitives provided by Java include `boolean`, `byte`, `char`, `double`, `float`, `int`, `long`, and `short`.

**private access**
An access-control characteristic applied to class members. Class members declared with the `private` access modifier are only accessible to code in the same class and are not inherited by subclasses.

**property**
A named characteristic or attribute of a type, class, or object.

**protected access**
An access-control characteristic applied to class members. Class members declared with the `protected` access modifier are accessible to code in the same class and package, and from code in subclasses, and they are inherited by subclasses.

**public access**
An access-control characteristic applied to interfaces, classes, and class members. Class members declared with the `public` access modifier are accessible anywhere the class is accessible and are inherited by subclasses. Classes and interfaces declared with the `public` access modifier are visible, accessible, and heritable outside of a package.

**qualifier**

A name or value used to locate or identify a particular entity within a set of similar entities.

**realization**

A relationship where one entity agrees to abide by or to carry out the contract specified by another entity.

**responsibility**

A purpose or obligation assigned to a type.

**role**

The set of responsibilities associated with an entity that participates in a specific relationship. A Java interface often defines a role for an object.

**service**

One or more operations provided by a type, class, or object to accomplish useful work on behalf of one or more clients.

**signature**

The name, parameter types, return type, and possible exceptions associated with an operation.

**state**

The condition or value of an object between events.

**static type checking**

Compile-time verification of the assumptions made about the use of object reference and data value types.

**subclass**

A class that inherits attributes and methods from another class.

**subtype**

The more specific type in a specialization–generalization relationship.

**superclass**

A class whose attributes and methods are inherited by another class.

**supertype**

The more general type in a specialization–generalization relationship.

**synchronization**

The process or mechanism used to preserve the invariant states of a program or object in the presence of multiple threads.

**synchronized**

A characteristic of a method or a block of code. A synchronized method or block allows only one thread at a time to execute within the *critical section* defined by that method or block.

**thread**

A single flow of control flow within a process that executes a sequence of instructions in an independent execution context.

**type**

Defines the common responsibilities, behavior, and operations associated with a set of similar objects. A type does not define an implementation.

**unchecked exception**

Any exception that is derived from `java.lang.RuntimeException` or `java.lang.Error`. A method that throws, or is a recipient of, an unchecked exception is not required to handle the exception or declare the exception in its `throws` clause.

**variable**

A typed, named container for holding object references or a data values.

**visibility**

The degree to which an entity may be accessed from outside of a particular scope.

# Bibliography

Ambler, S. W. *The Object Primer: The Application Developer's Guide to Object Orientation, second edition.* New York: SIGS Books/Cambridge University Press, 1995. ISBN 0-521-78519-7.

Ambler, S. W. *Building Object Applications That Work: Your Step-By-Step Handbook for Developing Robust Systems with Object Technology.* New York: SIGS Books/Cambridge University Press, 1998. ISBN 0-521-64826-2.

Ambler, S. W. *Process Patterns—Building Large-Scale Systems Using Object Technology.* New York: SIGS Books/Cambridge University Press, 1998. ISBN 0-521-64568-9.

Ambler, S. W. *More Process Patterns—Delivering Large-Scale Systems Using Object Technology.* New York: SIGS Books/Cambridge University Press, 1999. ISBN 0-521-65262-6.

Arnold, K. and J. Gosling. *The Java™ Programming Language.* Reading, Massachusetts: Addison–Wesley, 1996. ISBN 0-201-63455-4.

Chan, P. et al. *The Java™ Class Libraries, Volume 1: java.io, java.lang, java.math, java.net, java.text, java.util, 2nd Edition.* Reading, Massachusetts: Addison–Wesley, 1998. ISBN 0-201-31002-3.

Chan P. et al. *The Java™ Class Libraries, Volume 1: Supplement for the Java™ 2 Platform, Standard Edition, v1.2, 2nd Edition.* Reading, Massachusetts: Addison–Wesley, 1999. ISBN 0-201-48552-4.

Chan, P. and R. Lee. *The Java™ Class Libraries, Volume 2: java.applet, java.awt, java.beans, 2nd Edition*. Reading, Massachusetts: Addison–Wesley, 1998. ISBN 0-201-31003-1.

Gamma, E. et al. *Design Patterns: Elements of Reusable Object-Oriented Software*. Reading, Massachusetts: Addison–Wesley, 1995. ISBN 0-201-63361-2.

Gosling, J. et al. *The Java™ Language Specification*. Reading, Massachusetts: Addison–Wesley, 1996. ISBN 0-201-63451-1.

Kernighan, B. and P. J. Plauger. *The Elements of Programming Style, 2nd Edition*. New York: McGraw–Hill, June 1988. ISBN 0-07-034-207-5.

Lea, D. *Concurrent Programming in Java™: Design Principles and Patterns*. Reading, Massachusetts: Addison–Wesley, 1997. ISBN 0-201-69581-2.

Liskov, B. and J. Guttag. *Abstraction and Specification in Program Development*. New York: McGraw–Hill, 1986.

Maguire, S. *Writing Solid Code*. Redmond, Washington: Microsoft Press, 1993. ISBN 1-55615-4.

Martin, R. "Granularity," *C++ Report*, Vol. 8, No. 10 (Nov 1996), pp. 57–62. Accessed online at http://www.object mentor.com/publications/granularity.pdf, Aug 1999.

Martin, R. "Stability," *C++ Report*, Vol. 9, No. 2 (Feb 1997). Accessed online at http://www.objectmentor.com/publications/stability.pdf, Aug 1999.

McConnell, S. *Code Complete*. Redmond, Washington: Microsoft Press, 1993. ISBN 1-55615-484-4.

McConnell, S. *Software Project Survival Guide*. Redmond, Washington: Microsoft Press, 1998. ISBN 1-57231-621-7.

Meyer, B. *Object-Oriented Software Construction, 2nd Edition*. Englewood Cliffs, New Jersey: Prentice–Hall, Inc., 1997. ISBN 0-13-629155-4.

Nagler, J. "Coding Style and Good Computing Practices," *The Political Methodologist*, Spring 1995, Volume 6, No. 2.

Strunk, W., Jr., and E. B. White. *The Elements of Style*. New York: Macmillan, 1979. ISBN 0-02-418200-0.

Stroustrup, B. *The C++ Programming Language, 3rd Edition*. Reading, Massachusetts: Addison–Wesley, 1997. ISBN 0-201-88954-4.

Sun Microsystems, "Package Naming Conventions" In *Clarifications and Amendments to The Java™ Language Specification*. Palo Alto, California: Sun Microsystems, 26 Aug 1999. Accessed online at http://java.sun.com/docs/books/jls/clarify.html, Aug 1999.

Sun Microsystems, *JavaBeans™ API Specification.*, ed. G. Hamilton, Mountain View, California: Sun Microsystems Inc., 1997. Accessed online at http://www.javasoft.com/beans/docs/beans.101.pdf, Aug 1999.

Sun Microsystems, *Java™ Code Conventions*. Palo Alto, California: Sun Microsystems, 20 April 1999. Accessed online at ftp://ftp.javasoft.com/docs/codeconv/CodeConventions.pdf, Aug 1999.

Sun Microsystems, *JDK 1.2 API Documentation*. Palo Alto, California: Sun Microsystems, 1999. Accessed online at http://java.sun.com/products/jdk/1.2/docs/index.html, Aug 1999.

Taligent Press, *Taligent's Guide to Designing Programs*. Reading, Massachusetts: Addison–Wesley, 1994. ISBN 0-201-40888-0

# Index